THE PHILOSOPHY OF SIN

Oswald Chambers' Publications—

The Philosophy of Sin

and other Studies in the Problems of
Man's Moral Life

by
Oswald Chambers

OSWALD CHAMBERS PUBLICATIONS
ASSOCIATION

and

MARSHALL MORGAN & SCOTT

MARSHALL MORGAN & SCOTT
3 BEGGARWOOD LANE, BASINGSTOKE,
HANTS, UK

This edition (paperback) 1975
Reissued 1985

ISBN 0 551 05511 1

Printed photolitho in Great Britain by J. W. Arrowsmith Ltd., Bristol

CONTENTS

FOREWORD

The Philosophy of Sin is a subject of perennial interest, because the dreadful fact of sin is always with us. In every age there are the plain signs of some disruptive force at work among men. Hearts are being broken, lives are being spoiled, humanity is overclouded. Our Christian Faith sees that the underlying cause is Man's sin—his fundamental dislocation from God, with all its bitter consequences. A book like this, dealing with sin and its remedy, is to be welcomed, for it helps us to a clearer understanding of what is wrong with humankind, and of how the basic wrong can be put right —through Christ's Atonement making possible Man's repentance and appropriating faith. The salvation that *blots out sin* is here disclosed. "Sin is the radical twist with a supernatural originator, and salvation is a radical readjustment with a supernatural Originator." That is Good News indeed to every sinner ; and every man finds out at last that he is that, if he is a seeker after the truth. There are many other matters treated here. There are problems of conscience, of outward conduct, of the emotional life, the intellect, the bodily life, of circumstances, nerves, spiritual reality, the natural instincts, and of true inward adjustment to God. No one can ponder these themes as here treated without profit. The one great aim is to show modern Christians the way to the high levels of true holiness and righteousness, so that we may well use Dora Greenwell's prayer,

> " ' And Oh, that He fulfilled may see
> The travail of His soul in me
> And with His work contented be,
> As I with my dear Saviour ! ' "

D. L.

THE PHILOSOPHY OF SIN

"Departure from God's love is the common nature of all sin; and when the departure from this love was associated with a desire to progress in the direction of a selfishly appointed end, rather than of the end divinely appointed, this was the common nature of the primal sin of the world-spirit and of humanity."

The Bible is the only Book that tells us anything about the originator of sin. There is a difference between an experimental knowledge of sin and an intellectual understanding of what sin is. We seem to be built on the following plan: at first we experience a need, then we hunt for the satisfaction of that need; when the need is supplied we turn our whole nature in the direction of an explanation of how the need was supplied. When we are convicted of sin, we are convicted of the need of a Saviour; and we seek for the Saviour intellectually and in various other ways till we meet with our Lord by the power of His Spirit and experience salvation; then comes the great need we are trying to insist on in these talks, the need of turning the whole nature to understand how God supplied the need. That is what Christians are neglecting, they have the experience but they have left their minds to stagnate, they have not turned back again and tried to find out what God reveals about sin, about salvation, and about the whole life of man. According to the Bible, God is only manifested at the last point; when a man is driven by personal experience to the last limit, he is apt to meet God. The same thing is true in thinking, we can do very well without God in thinking as long as we think only as splendid animals. As long as we are not at the last place, not facing our problems at all, but simply pleased to be in existence, pleased to be healthy and happy, we will never find God, we do not see any need for Him. But when we are driven in thinking to the last limit, then we begin to find that God manifests Himself there. To people who are satisfied on too shallow a level the Bible is a book of impertinences, but whenever human nature is driven to the end of things, then the Bible becomes the only Book and God the only Being in the world.

(1) THE MASKED ORIGIN OF SATAN'S PRIMAL SIN. (Isaiah xiv. 12–15.)

We are dealing not so much with the experience of sin as with the light God's Word throws on how sin began; we must have a basis for thinking. If we have been delivered from sin by the power of God within us, thank God for it; but there is something more than that, we have now to allow God to illuminate our darkness by His revelation.

We take this passage in Isaiah as the early Christian fathers did, as an exposition of Satan behind his material puppets. One of the significant things the Bible reveals about Satan is that he rarely works without being incarnated. (*See* Genesis iii. 15, *and* Matthew xvi. 23.) God's Spirit and our Lord trace Satan behind men and women who are really time-manifestations of Satan. That is the region in which we are to look for the obscure origin of sin; it does not look as if sin came in that way at all. Only when we are driven to extremes do we realize that the Bible is the only Book that gives us any indication of the true nature of sin, and where it came from.

(*a*) *Marvellous Originator of Sin*. (*v.* 12.) An angel next in power to God is revealed to be the originator of sin.

(*b*) *Mystic Order of Revolt*. (*v.* 13.) In this verse the Mystic Order of Satan's Revolt is revealed, it was a purely spiritual revolt against God.

(*c*) *Mad Outrival of God*. (*v.* 14.) A determination to outrival God.

These three points are nonsense unless we are driven to the last limit. The fact that people ridicule the belief in Satan and sin is simply an indication of the principle we have laid down, that we do not see God till we get to the last point and His Word has no meaning for us until we get there; but when the soul of man is driven to the last lap of trying to find out things, then the Bible becomes the only Book there is, and this 'theory,' as men call it, is seen to be the revelation of God about the origin of sin. Sin is that factor in human nature which has a supernatural originator who stands next to God in power. The sin of Satan is revealed only dimly, but the dim outline indicates that it was the summit of all sin, full, free, conscious, spiritual sin; he was not entrapped into it, he was not ensnared into it, he sinned with the full clear understanding of what he was doing. We know that much, so far the veil is transparent.

(2) THE MASKED OUTGUARDS OF SATAN'S PRIMAL SNARE. (Genesis iii. 6–7.)

Satan guards the main body of his purpose; neither Eve nor Adam had the slightest notion who he was; he was as far removed in his first snare from his real body of intent as could possibly be. We have to remember that God created Adam 'a son of God,' and God required Adam to develop himself by obeying Him; that obedience necessarily involved the sacrifice of the natural life to transform it into spiritual life, and this was to be done by a series of moral choices. Satan lays his first snare there, the first outguard of his snare is away altogether from the main body of his purpose, he does not reveal what he is after in the beginning.

(a) *Soul stained by Natural Interest.* Verse 6 reveals that Satan was part of God's natural creation, he spoke to the woman first, who represented all we understand by the affinities of a human soul for the natural life, unsuspecting, unsuspicious, sympathetic and curious. In looking at sin in its beginnings, we find its true nature in all its working. Our Lord spoke about men as sheep; a sheep has no set conscious purpose to go wrong, it simply wanders; and our Lord used the illustration for men; the majority of men wander like sheep without any conscious bad intent at all. That is the first outwork or outguard of Satan, he gets us all here like silly stupid sheep; he has never altered his way of working, and although it is written clearly in God's Book, we never seem to be forewarned that the soul is stained through natural interest.

(b) *Soul snared by Natural Intimacy.* (v. 6.) The two

11

intimacies indicated in *v.* 6 are, first, intimacy with the object desired, and, second, intimacy with the closest vital relationship; when Eve saw the food was good she fetched her husband. To sin alone is never possible. In writing of Eve, Paul says that Satan 'beguiled' her, meaning by that that there was no clear understanding on her part of the wrong she had done; but "Adam was not beguiled." "He did eat" (Genesis iii. 6). Adam's sin was the perfect conscious realization of what he was doing.

(*c*) *Soul sin by Natural Influence.* (*v.* 7.) Adam was required by God to take part in his own development, i.e. he had to transform the life of nature into the spiritual life by obeying God. The life of nature is neither moral nor immoral; our bodies are neither moral nor immoral, we make them moral or immoral. Our Lord had a body, and we read that He hungered; it was not a sin for Him to be hungry, but it would have been a sin for Him to have eaten during the forty days in the wilderness, because His Father's word at that time was that He should not eat. It is not a sin to have a body, to have natural appetites, but it is a sin to refuse to sacrifice them at the word of God. Satan's first fundamental outguards are in the innocence of nature. We say, 'But it cannot be wrong to have a little sympathy here, a little curiosity there'; the Bible lifts the veil just enough to show there is a great supernatural force behind that entices for one purpose, to get us away from obeying God's voice.

(3) The Masked Overset of Spiritual Surrender. (Genesis iii. 1–7.)

Satan succeeded in putting his outguards so far away from the main body of his purpose that no one but God Himself knew what he was doing. Unsuspecting Eve was as far removed from understanding what Satan was doing as we are when we sin, but where both are culpable in every respect is in the refusal to obey God; and whenever there is a refusal to obey God, instantly Satan's first snare is entered into. When once the first snare has caught us we are done for, the rest is as easy as can be; once let the principle of refusing to sacrifice the life of nature to the will of God have way, and all the rest happens easily.

(a) *Infused Suspicion of the Innermost.* (v. 1.) It was the internal region of man, the innermost, that yielded first; bodily action was last; the first thing that yielded was the mind. The Bible reveals that human nature possesses an incurable suspicion of God. Its origin is explained in the Bible; two great primal creatures of God, the angel who became Satan, and Adam, negotiated a relationship which God never sanctioned. That was how sin was introduced into the world. As long as we live on the surface of things merely as splendid animals, we shall find the Bible nonsense. We are reverent over the Bible simply because our fathers and mothers taught us to be reverent; but we find no practical reason for reverence until we get to the last lap, until we are pressed out of the outer court into the inner, then we find there is no mind among men that has ever penned words that are sufficient for us there; we begin to find that the only Book there is the Bible. When we get to the last point the only exact counterpart for our natural life is this Book.

When the Bible touches the question of sin, it always comes right down to this incurable suspicion of God which never can be altered apart from the Atonement because it is connected with a great supernatural power behind. Paul talks about it and calls it the "carnal mind," he does not say it is at enmity with God, because that might mean it could be cured; he says it *is* "enmity against God." Remember the summit of all sin was a conscious red-handed revolt against God. Adam's sin was not a conscious revolt against God; it worked out ultimately through the race as a revolt against God, but Adam's sin instead of being at the summit of all sin is at the foundation of all sin. Consequently whatever sin you take, you will get the characteristics that were in this first sin, viz., the principle and the disposition of this infused suspicion, "Yea, hath God said . . ." (Genesis iii. 1–5.) Absolute devastation awaits the soul that

13

allows suspicion to creep in. Suspicion of God is like a gap in a dyke, the flood rushes through, nothing can stop it. The first thing you will do is to accept slanders against God. Because it is peculiar to you? No, because it is according to the stock that runs right straight through the human race, from this first sin of infused suspicion in the intelligence, in the innermost part of man.

The majority of us prefer to trust our innocence rather than the statements of Jesus. It is always risky to trust your innocence when the statements of Jesus are contrary to it. Jesus says that "from within, out of the heart of men proceed . . .", then comes the awful catalogue. You say, 'Why, that is nonsense, I never had any of those things in my heart, I am innocent.' Some day you will come up against a set of circumstances which will prove that your innocence was a figment, and that what Jesus said about the human heart was perfectly true.

(b) *Irresistible Sensuality of the Inner.* (v. 5.) Once allow suspicion of God and of His goodness and justice to enter into a man's mind and the floodgates of sensuality are opened. We mean by 'sensuality,' the life that draws its sustenance from natural surroundings, guided by a selfishly appointed purpose. We used to mean by sensuality gross awful and shocking sins; the word means that but a great deal more. Sensuality may be refined down to the thinness of a cloud. It is quite possible to be grossly sensual and spiritual. It is possible to say, 'I have one desire in being good, in being saved and sanctified, a particular end of my own'; that is sensuality. Once suspicion of God is allowed to come in, there is no limit to the flood of sensuality. Lust, too, is a word that the Bible uses in a different way. We use the word lust for the gross abominable sins of the flesh only, but the Bible uses it for a great deal more than that. Lust simply means, 'I must have this at once'; it may be a bodily appetite or a spiritual possession. The principle lust works on is, 'I must have it at once, I cannot wait for God's time, God is too indifferent,' that is the way lust works. Watch how our Lord faced men, He

14

always faced this disposition of sin, He never summed men up by their external conduct. He was not driven into panics by immorality and fleshly sordidness, that sort of sin never seemed to bother Him half as much as the respectable pride of men and women who never were guilty of those things. The mainspring of such lives is a wise judicious working which keeps all outward circumstances in harmony with the one ruling desire. The soul, remember, is simply the spirit of a man expressing itself. The spirit of a child can rarely express itself, the soul has not become articulate. 'Soul' in the Bible nearly always refers to the fleshly nature, it is the only power a man has for expressing his true spirit. "God is always manifested in the ultimates" (Goethe). That is what we mean by saying that God is only revealed at the last point. If we are only living on the surface of things the Bible line will appear stupid, but if we have had a dose of 'the plague of our own heart,' and realize what God has delivered us from, we know much too much ever to accept man's definition of sin, we know that there is no other explanation than the Bible one, and nothing but pity is awakened when we hear people trying to explain sin apart from the Bible.

(c) *Iniquitous Succumbing of the Individual.* (*v. 7.*) 'Iniquitous' means an unjust and unequal twisting; and 'individual' means here the whole person going out in a definite act. Suspicion first, sensuality next, and manifest ruin last. If sin is a radical twist with a supernatural originator, salvation is a radical readjustment with a supernatural Originator. To present salvation as less than that is deplorable. If all Jesus Christ can do is to run a parallel counter-action with what Satan can do, His right name is 'Culture,' not 'Saviour'; but His revealed nature was stated by the angel to Mary, and repeated over and over again, "Thou shalt call His name Jesus, *for He shall save His people from their sins.*" The slight views of salvation, the sympathetic drifty views that all Jesus Christ can do is to put in us a principle that counteracts another principle, will cause anyone who has got to the last limit to blaspheme God for a

15

thing like that. It all comes from a flimsy, wrong view of sin. If that is all He can do, what is the good of calling Him Saviour? No one who has ever faced sin in its reality would ever give one cent for that kind of salvation, it is nothing but the exalting of education, culture will do that, or cunning. When you come to the New Testament and to your own experience you find that salvation is as radical as sin, and if God has not radically altered your heredity, thank God you may know He can by the power of Jesus Christ's Atonement. It is only the right view of sin and right thinking about sin that ever will explain Jesus Christ's Life and Death and Resurrection. It is sin that He came to cope with; He did not come to cope with the poor little mistakes of men, they cope with their own mistakes; He came to give them a totally new stock of heredity, that is, He came to implant into them His own nature, so that Satan's power in the soul is absolutely destroyed, not counteracted.

When God has put His Spirit in you and identified you with Jesus Christ, what is to be your attitude to your bodily life? You have the same body, the same appetites and the same nature as before, your members used to be servants of sin; but Jesus Christ is your Example now. He sacrificed Himself to His Father's will, see that you do the same as a saint. He submitted His intelligence to His Father's will, see that you do the same as a saint. He submitted His will to His Father, see that you as a saint do the same. Jesus Christ did all that Adam failed to do. Satan met our Lord with his masked outguards exactly as he met Adam, and the Spirit of God drove Jesus into the wilderness to meet these outguards of Satan. "If Thou be the Son of God . . ." Satan tried to insinuate the first suspicion, but it would not work, Jesus refused to be suspicious of God. He overcame by obeying the word of His Father, that is, He transformed His natural life into a spiritual life by obeying the voice of God, and as saints we have to obey Jesus Christ and sacrifice the life of nature to His will.

EDUCATIVE INSIGHT INTO REDEMPTION

"How much more shall the blood of Christ, who through the eternal Spirit offered Himself without blemish unto God, cleanse our conscience from dead works to serve the living God?"

(Hebrews ix. 14.)

(1) TRUE TO THE CROSS.

As we go on with God the Holy Spirit brings us back more and more to the one absorbing theme of the New Testament, viz. the death of the Lord Jesus Christ and its meaning from His standpoint. Our right to ourselves in every shape and form was destroyed once and for ever by the death of Jesus, and we have to be educated into the realization of what this means in all its fulness. We have to come to a relationship to the Cross in thought as well as in life.

"How much more . . ." How much more is there to know, for instance, after sanctification? Everything! Before sanctification we know nothing, we are simply put in the place of knowing; that is, we are led *up* to the Cross; in sanctification we are led *through* the Cross—for what purpose? For a life of outpouring service to God. The characteristic of a saint after identification with the death of Jesus is that he is brought down from the ineffable glory of the heavenly places into the valley to be crushed and broken in service for God. We are here with no right to ourselves, for no spiritual blessing for ourselves; we are here for one purpose only—to be made servants of God as Jesus was. Have we as saints allowed our minds to be brought face to face with this great truth? The death of Jesus not only gives us remission from our sins, it enables us to assimilate the very nature of Jesus until in every detail of our lives we are like Him. "How much more" does the death of Jesus mean to us to-day than it ever has before? Are we beginning to be lost in wonder, love

17

and praise at the marvellous loosening from sin, and are we so assimilating the nature of Jesus that we bear a strong family likeness to Him?

"shall the blood of Christ . . ." It was not the blood of a martyr, not the blood of goats and calves, that was shed, but "the blood of Christ." The very life of God was shed for the world—"the church of God which He purchased with His own blood." (Acts xx. 28.) All the perfections of the essential nature of God were in that blood; all the holiest attainments of man were in that blood. The death of Jesus reaches away down underneath the deepest sin human nature ever committed. This aspect of the death of Jesus takes us into a spiritual domain beyond the threshold of the thinking of the majority of us. The cry on the Cross, "My God, My God, why hast Thou forsaken Me?" is unfathomable to us. The only ones—and I want to say this very deliberately—the only ones who come near the threshold of understanding the cry of Jesus are not the martyrs, they knew that God had not forsaken them, His presence was so wonderful; not the lonely missionaries who are killed or forsaken, they experience exultant joy, for God is with them when men forsake them: the only ones who come near the threshold of understanding the experience of God-forsakenness are men like Cain—"My punishment is greater than I can bear;" men like Esau, ". . . an exceeding bitter cry;" men like Judas. Jesus Christ knew and tasted to a fuller depth than any man could ever taste what it is to be separated from God by sin. If Jesus Christ was a martyr, our salvation is a myth. We have followed cunningly devised fables if Jesus Christ is not all that this cry represents Him to be—the Incarnate God becoming identified with sin in order to save men from hell and damnation. The depth of this cry of Jesus is deeper than any man can go because it is a cry from the heart of God. The height and depth of our salvation are only measured by God Almighty on His throne and Jesus Christ in the heart of hell. The most devout among us are too flippant about this great subject of the death of Jesus Christ. When we stand before the

18

Cross, is our every commonplace pious mood stripped off, or do we get caught up by the modern spirit and think of the Cross only as delivering us from sin, or as a type of sanctification? Thank God for salvation through the Cross, for sanctification through the Cross; but thank God also for insight into what it cost God to make that salvation and sanctification possible. God grant that the pulsing power of identification with the death of Jesus may come again into our testimony and make it glow with devotion to Him for His unspeakable salvation.

"Who through the eternal Spirit . . ." The life of Jesus portrays the handiwork of the Holy Spirit; we know what the Holy Spirit will be in us if we let Him have His way. The underlying consciousness of Jesus was the Eternal God Himself; the Eternal Spirit was behind all He did. It is not so with us. There is a fundamental difference as well as a similarity between the Spirit in Jesus and the Spirit in us. The Eternal Spirit was incarnated in Jesus; He never is in us. By regeneration and sanctification He energizes our spirits and brings us into oneness with Jesus Christ, so that our underlying consciousness is "hid with Christ in God." We are only made acceptable to God by relying on the Eternal Spirit Who was incarnated absolutely in Jesus Christ. The Spirit in us will never allow us to forget that the death of Jesus was the death of God Incarnate. "God was in Christ reconciling the world unto Himself." (2 Cor. v. 19.)

"offered Himself without blemish unto God . . ." Who offered Himself? The Son of God. He was immaculate, without blemish, yet He was crucified. This rules out once and for ever the conception that Jesus died the death of a martyr; He died a death no martyr could touch. He died the death not of a good man but of a bad man, with the vicarious pain of Almighty God in His heart.

Our hearts are wrung with pathos when we read of the offering of Isaac and the sacrifice of Jephthah's daughter, for they are unbearably pathetic. The offering of Jesus is not pathetic in the tiniest degree; it is beyond all pathos.

There is something infinitely profounder than pathos in the death of Jesus; there is a mystery we cannot begin to touch. The death of Jesus is the death of God, at the hands of man, inspired by the devil. He gathered round Him the raging hate of humanity, and was crucified. He offered Himself through the Eternal Spirit—He died in the Spirit in which He lived.

Are we being true to the Cross in our preaching, putting first the holiness of God that makes men know that they are sinners? When we preach the love of God there is a danger of forgetting that the Bible reveals not first the love of God but the intense, blazing holiness of God, with His love as the centre of that holiness. When the holiness of God is preached, men are convicted of sin; it is not the love of God that first appeals but His holiness. The awful nature of the conviction of sin that the Holy Spirit brings makes us realize that God cannot, dare not, must not forgive sin; if God forgave sin without atoning for it our sense of justice would be greater than His.

(2) TRUE TO CONSCIENCE.

How does all the profound thought underlying the death of Jesus touch us? The writer to the Hebrews instantly connects it with conscience—"How much more shall the blood of Christ, . . . cleanse our conscience from dead works to serve the living God?" Has conscience the place in our salvation and sanctification that it ought to have? Hyper-conscientious people blind themselves to the realization of what the death of Jesus means by saying, 'No, I have wronged this person and I must put the thing right.' It springs from the panging remorse that we experience when we realize we have wronged another. 'All you say about the Cross may be true, but I have been so mean and so wrong that there are things I must put right first.' It sounds noble to talk like that, but it is the essence of the pride that put Jesus Christ to death. The only thing to do is to cast the whole thing aside: 'My God, this thing in me is worthy only of death, the awful death of crucifixion to the last strand of life. Lord, it is my sin, my wrong, not Jesus Christ, that ought to be on that Cross.' When we get there and abandon the whole thing, the blood of Christ cleanses our conscience and the freedom is ineffable and amazing.

The greatest problems of conscience are not the wrong things we have done, but wrong relationships. We may have become born again, but what about those we have wronged? It is of no use to sit down and say, 'It is irreparable now, I cannot alter it.' Thank God He can alter it! We may try to repair the damage in our own way, by apologizing, by writing letters; but it is not a simple easy matter of something to apologize for. Behind the veil of human lives God begins to reveal the tragedies of hell. Or we may say, 'I have been atoned for, therefore I do not need to think about the past.' If we are conscientious, the Holy Spirit will make us think about the past, and it is just here that the tyranny of nerves and the bondage of Satan comes in. The shores of life are strewn with ruined friendships, irreparable severances through our own blame or others, and when the Holy Spirit begins to reveal the tremendous twist, then comes the strange distress, 'How can we repair it?' Many a sensitive soul has been driven into insanity through anguish of mind because he has never realized what Jesus Christ came to do, and all the asylums in the world will never touch them in the way of healing; the only thing that will is the realization of what the death of Jesus means, viz. that the damage we have done may be repaired through the efficacy of His Cross. Jesus Christ has atoned for all, and He can make it good in us, not only as a gift but by a participation on our part. The miracle of the grace of God is that He can make the past as though it had never been; He can "restore the years that the locust hath eaten, the cankerworm, and the caterpiller, and the palmerworm" (Joel ii. 25).

How Jesus Christ does cleanse our conscience! It is freedom not only from sin and the damage sin has done, but emancipation from the impairing left by sin, from all the distortions left in mind and imagination. Then when our conscience has been cleansed from dead works, Jesus Christ gives us the marvellously healing ministry of intercession as "a clearing-house for conscience." Not only is all sense of past guilt removed, but we are given the very secret heart of God for the purpose of vicarious intercession (*see* Romans viii. 26–7).

"from dead works . . ." What are 'dead works'? Everything done apart from God. All prayer, all preaching, all testifying, all kind, sacrificial deeds done apart from God, are dead works that clog the life. Never forget for one moment that you are what you are by the grace of God. If you are not what you are by the grace of God, then may God have mercy on you! Everything we are that is not through the grace of God will be a dead clog on us. Oh believe me, the curse of the saint is his goodness! Let the whole thing go, be true to the Cross, and let Jesus Christ cleanse your conscience from dead works. Many saints misunderstand what happens to the natural virtues after sanctification. The natural virtues are not promises of what we are going to be, but remnants of what God created man to be. We have the idea that we can bank on our natural patience and truthfulness and conscientiousness; we can bank on nothing in heaven above or earth beneath but what the grace of God has wrought in us. Everything we possess in the way of moral property, of noble spiritual property, severs us from God; all must go. "Nothing in my hands I bring . . ." Immediately we abandon like that, we experience what Paul says in Galatians ii. 20—"I have been crucified with Christ," and the reconstruction of our lives proves that God has cleansed us from all dead works.

"to serve the living God." This means a life laid down for Jesus, a life of narrowed interests, a life that deliberately allows itself to be swamped by a crowd of paltry things. It is not fanaticism, it is the stedfast, flint-like attitude of heart and mind and body for one purpose—spoilt for everything saving as we can be used to win souls for Jesus.

22

It is not "a passion for souls," but something infinitely profounder than that it is the passion of the Holy Ghost for Jesus Christ. There are things that are too humanly tender for this kind of service. There are lives prevented by claims that are not God's, prevented by the tender, passionate love of others who have come in between. Oh the amount of wasted service for God, the agonies of weeping and self-pity, the margins of mourning over wasted opportunities! Jesus Christ never spent one moment of His life mourning in that way. The kind of things we grieve over is the evidence of where our life is hid. Some of us have a social conscience, we are shocked at moral crime; some of us have a religious conscience, we are shocked at the things that go against our creeds. The conscience formed in us by the Holy Spirit makes us amazingly sensitive to the things that tell against the honour of God.

I am convinced that what is needed in spiritual matters is reckless abandonment to the Lord Jesus Christ, reckless and uncalculating abandonment, with no reserve anywhere about it; not sad, you cannot be sad if you are abandoned absolutely. Are you thankful to God for your salvation and sanctification, thankful He has purged your conscience from dead works? Then go a step further; let Jesus Christ take you straight through into identification with His death until there is nothing left but the light at the foot of the Cross, and the whole sphere of the life is hid with Christ in God.

SALVATION

"Ye that have escaped the sword, go ye, stand not still; remember the Lord from afar and let Jerusalem come into your mind." *Jeremiah* li. 50.

Salvation is the biggest, gladdest word in the world; it cannot mean pretence in any shape or form, therefore suppression is no element of the word, neither is counteraction. Salvation is God's grace to sinful men, and it takes a lifetime to say the word properly. Most of us restrict the meaning of salvation, we use it to mean New Birth only, or something limited. We are dealing with the subject here practically, not theologically.

(1) THE ELEMENT OF DESTRUCTION IN SALVATION. "Ye that have escaped the sword."

The 51st chapter of Jeremiah almost burns the page, it is so full of strong and intense destruction; but it gives the keynote to the purpose of God in destruction, viz. the deliverance of the good. You will never find in the Bible that things are destroyed for the sake of destruction. Human beings destroy for the sake of destruction, and so does the devil; God never does, He destroys the wrong and the evil for one purpose only, the deliverance of the good.

(a) *The Purpose of the Sword.* The purpose of the sword is to destroy everything that hinders a man being delivered. The first thing in salvation is the element of destruction, and it is this that men object to. With this thought in mind, recall what our Lord said about His own mission: "Think not that I am come to send peace on earth: I came not to send peace, but a sword" (Matt. x. 34). Our Lord reveals Himself as the destroyer of all peace and happiness, and of ignorance, wherever these are the cloke for sin (cf. Matt. iii. 10). It sounds a startling and amazing thing to say that Jesus did not come to send peace, but He said

24

He did not. The one thing Jesus Christ is after is the destruction of everything that would hinder the emancipation of men. The fact that people are happy and peaceful and prosperous is no sign that they are free from the sword of God. If their happiness and peace and well-being and complacency rests on an undelivered life, they will meet the sword before long, and all their peace and rest and joy will be destroyed.

(b) *The Peril of the Sword.* To say that 'God loves the sinner, but hates his sin' sounds all right, but it is a dangerous statement, because it means that God is far too loving ever to punish the sinner. Jesus Christ came to save us so that there should be no 'sinner' left in us. The phrase 'a sinner saved by grace' means that a man is no longer a sinner; if he is, he is not saved. If I refuse to let God destroy my sin, there is only one possible result—I must be destroyed with my sin. The light of the Lord's presence convicts of sin. (See John xv. 22–4.) Sin is never imputed unless it is conscious. These verses reveal the very essence of the destructive element of salvation. I can easily say I am not convicted of sin; but immediately I stand face to face with Jesus Christ I know the difference between Him and myself; I have no cloke and no excuse, and if I refuse to allow the Lord to deliver me from all that He reveals, I shall be destroyed with the thing He came to destroy. "To this end was the Son of God manifested, that He might destroy the works of the devil" (1 John iii. 8).

(c) *The Power of the Sword.* An ancient legend tells of a blacksmith who became famous for the magnificent swords he made; he claimed that they could cut a coat of armour in two with one sweep. The king hearing of this boast, summoned the blacksmith to his presence and told him to cut through his coat of armour and if he could not do it, he would be put to death for his boasting. The blacksmith swung his sword round and put it back in its sheath; the king was about to challenge him, when the blacksmith said, 'Shake yourself, your majesty'; the king shook himself, and fell in two. The legend is an illustration of the tremendous

25

power of the sword in God's hands, "the sword of the Spirit, which is the word of God." "The word of God is sharper than any two-edged sword," and it deals effectually with the sin in us; for a while we may not be conscious that anything has happened, then suddenly God brings about a crisis and we realize that something has been profoundly altered. No one is ever the same after listening to the word of God, you cannot be; you may imagine you have paid no attention to it, and yet months after maybe a crisis arises and suddenly the word of God comes and grips you by the throat, so to speak, and awakens all the terrors of hell in your life, and you say, 'Wherever did that word come from?' Years ago, months ago, weeks ago, it sank straight into your unconscious mind, God knew it was there though you did not, and it did its damaging work, and now it has suddenly come to light. The question is, will you allow yourself to escape the edge of the sword, or will you be destroyed with the thing the sword has pierced?

Look back over your own life and examine the points of view you have now and the points of view you once had. At one time you were violently opposed to the views you now hold; what has altered you? You cannot honestly say it was conscious study. God says that His word shall not return unto Him void (Isaiah lv. 10–11)—the abiding success of the word of God! The word of God is never without power, and as a servant or handmaid of God you have nothing whatever to do with whether people dislike and reject the word of God, or 'purr' over it. See you preach it no matter what they think of you, that is a matter of absolute indifference, sooner or later the effect of that word will be manifested. The great snare is to seek acceptance with the people we talk to, to give people only what they want; we have no business to wish to be acceptable to the people we teach. "Study to show thyself approved"—unto the saints? No, "unto God." I have never known a man or woman who taught God's word to be always acceptable to other people. As a worker for God truths are all the time coming into your own life which you would never have seen for yourself, and as

26

you give other people truths they never saw before, they will say—'I don't agree with that.' It is foolish to begin to argue, if it is God's truth leave it alone; let mistakes correct themselves. When a crisis comes that shakes the life, they will find the old dominating power is not there at all. What has happened? The destruction of God has gone on. Then comes the critical moment, will I go with the thing that is destroyed, or will I stay by the hand that holds the sword?

"The best measure of the profundity of any religious doctrine is given by its conception of sin and its cure of sin."

Do I believe that sin needs to be corrected or killed? If sin only needed to be corrected, the symbol would have been a lash, not a sword; but God uses the symbol for killing. Beware of getting into your mind ideas which never came from God's word, the idea, for instance, that we sin a little less each day; if we do, the salvation of Jesus Christ has never touched us. If we grow in grace a little more every day, it is a sign that the destructive power of God has been at work, and that we have been delivered from the thing that hindered us growing. The view men have of sin is always the test of their view of salvation, and to-day views are creeping into God's Book that never came from Him. Sin must be destroyed, not corrected; it is the destruction of something in order to lead to emancipation. It is always God rescuing Israel from Babylon; always Jesus Christ rescuing His people from their sin.

(2) THE ELEMENT OF DIRECTION IN SALVATION. "Go ye, stand not still."

To study the teaching of our Lord in connection with the verb "to go" would amaze us. How often do you hear in meetings the word "go," and how often do you hear the word "get"? We emphasize "get"; the New Testament emphasizes "go." If you have escaped the edge of the sword, go!

27

(a) *The Paralysis of Sin.* Slaves born in slavery and suddenly freed, will often prefer to go back. When the slaves in America were freed, they did not know what to do with their freedom, they were amazed and dazed and stupid, they had never been master of themselves before, and many pleaded with their masters to be taken back. That moment of paralysis is the natural result of being suddenly delivered. A sinner when first delivered from sin has such moments, he wishes God would take him safe to heaven where he would be secure from temptation. We may not say it, but it is common to us all to look at things in this way in the implicit region, if not in the explicit—'Yes, I believe God does deliver from sin and fill with the Holy Spirit, and if He would only take me straight to heaven it would be all right, but I have to live amongst people who are wrong, in the midst of a people of unclean lips and the memory of how continually I fell in the past makes me fear I shall do it again in the future.' Satan takes advantage of these moments of paralysis; consequently there is need for direction. A snare in many evangelistic meetings is that people are taught to say, 'Thank God, I am saved,' or, 'Thank God I am sanctified,' but no line of direction is given. The counsel in God's Book is—Testify to the truth God has revealed to you, and *go on.* People begin to degenerate because they don't know what to do; the direction given in God's Book has never been put in its right place. The direction is summed up in this one word, *Go.*

(b) *The Pain of the Saved.* When a limb that has long been cramped is released, there is the experience of excessive pain, but the pain is the sign of life. The first moment of realizing God's truth is usually a moment of ecstasy, the life is brimming over with joy and happiness and brightness, there is no pain, nothing but unspeakable, unfathomable joy. Then the verb "to go" begins to be conjugated, and we experience the 'growing pains' of salvation, and Satan comes as an angel of light and says, 'Don't go on, stand still, and,' in the language of the hymn, " 'sing yourself away to everlasting bliss!' "

28

We do not consider enough the necessity of learning how to walk spiritually. Remember, when we are saved, we have been cramped in sin. Paul puts it in this way—'You used to use your members as servants for sin, now you are emancipated from sin, use your members as servants to righteousness,' that is, use them in a different way. (*See* Romans vi. 19.) If a man has used his arm only for writing, and then becomes a blacksmith, he will groan for days with the tremendous pain in the deltoid muscle until by practice the time comes when there is no more pain because the muscle has become rightly adjusted to its new work. The same thing happens spiritually, God begins to teach us how to walk and over and over again we begin to howl and complain. May God save us from the continual whine of spiritual babes—'Teach us the same things over and over again, don't give us the revelations of God which are painful, give us the 'simple gospel,' i.e. what we have always believed, don't tell us of things we have never thought about before, because that causes pain' (cf. Hebrews v. 12). Of course it does. Thank God there is a pain attached to being saved, the pain of growing until we come to maturity where we can do the work of a son or daughter of God.

(c) *The Passion in the Saving.* The application of our Lord's phrase, "Behold, we go up to Jerusalem," is this passion not to stand still, but to go on. Look back over your life in grace, whether long or short, and ask yourself which are the days that have furthered you most in the knowledge of God—the days of sunshine and peace and prosperity? Never! The days of adversity, the days of strain, the days of sudden surprises, the days when the earthly house of this tabernacle was strained to its last limit, those are the days when you learned the meaning of this passion of "Go." Any great calamity in the natural world—death, disease, bereavement—will awaken a man when nothing else would, and he is never the same again. We would never know the 'treasures of darkness' if we were always in the place of placid security. Thank God, salvation does not mean that God turns us into milksops; God's salvation makes us for the first time into

29

men and women. The passion of the Holy Ghost means that we go on with God exactly on the lines God wants; the Holy Ghost will give the direction, and if we do not know it we are to blame. "My people doth not consider," says God; they won't heed this Book. We say, 'I don't like studying these subjects, I have no affinity for them.' We do not say it actually, but over and over again these thoughts keep us from going on with God. The Holy Spirit will make us face subjects for which we have no affinity naturally in order that we may become full-orbed as God's servants.

(3) THE ELEMENT OF DISCIPLINE IN SALVATION. "remember the Lord from afar, and let Jerusalem come into your mind."

In the midst of an alien land, afar off from the home of God, the remembrance of the Lord will make you strong with the strength of ten. Note carefully in this connection our Lord's use of the phrase "Do this in remembrance of Me." The ordinance of the Lord's Supper is not a memorial of One Who has gone, but of One Who is always here.

(a) *The Dangerous Infatuation*. Infatuation means a stupid sense of my own security. A sick person has often the dangerous infatuation that he is all right. This danger overtakes a saint on what Bunyan calls "the enchanted ground." (Cf. 2 Peter i. 12–13.) Whenever we come to the state of feeling, 'Well, it's all right now and I can rest here,' we are in danger. There is only one point of rest, and that is in the Lord, not in our experiences. We are never told to rest in the experience of salvation or of sanctification or in anything saving the Lord Himself. Whenever you rest in the dangerous infatuation, 'Thank God, I know I am all right,' you will go down as sure as Satan is Satan and you are you.

(b) *The Divine Imperative*. "Remember the Lord from afar." The command to remember does not simply mean to recall, but to re-identify yourself in imagination with your Lord. The passive stage is a great danger—

30

When obstacles and trials seem like prison walls to be,
I lay me down and go to sleep and leave it all to Thee!

That is the stage of spiritual dry rot. There is nothing more difficult to get rid of than the encroachments of this spiritual sickness; it is not physical weariness, that will come over and over again, but spiritual weariness, and spiritual weariness coins such phrases as "Once in grace always in grace, no matter how disgraceful you are." "The Lord is far too good to let me go." "I have been so much used in days gone by, I am all right." It is rather a certainty that you are spiritually sick. Jesus said, "I am come that they might have *life*," not laziness. Whenever we are in danger of nestling in spiritual armchairs, the clarion voice of the Lord comes and bids us neither "sit nor stand but go!" Look back over your life and you will see whenever there was the danger of spiritual dry rot or of getting off on to enchanted ground, God in mercy to your soul allowed an earthquake to come, and the whole thing went to pieces and you with it; for a while you were dazed and amazed, and then all of a sudden He set you on your feet again. "For we have not here an abiding city." To "remember the Lord from afar" means to remember that we have to be like Him.

(c) *The Devoted Intellect.* "And let Jerusalem," the God-lit city, "come into your mind." Ask yourself—'What do I let come into my mind?' If a man lets his garden alone, it pretty soon ceases to be a garden; and if a saint lets his mind alone, it will soon become a garbage patch for Satan's scarecrows. Read the terrible things that Paul says will grow in the mind of a saint unless he looks after it (e.g. Col. iii. 5). The command to let Jerusalem come into our mind means we have to watch our intellect and devote it for one purpose; let only those things come in that are worthy of the God-lit city. *"Let"* . . . it is a command. See to it by the careful watching of your mind that only those thoughts come in that are worthy of God. We do not sufficiently realize the need to pray when we lie down at night, "Deliver us from the evil one." It puts us in the attitude of asking the Lord to watch our minds and our dreams, and He will do it.

REALITY

It seems to me that somewhere in my soul
   There lies a secret self as yet asleep;
   No stranger hath disturbed its slumber deep,
No friend dispersed the clouds that round it roll.
But it is written on my Fortune's scroll
   That should some hand the chords of being sweep
   And speak a certain sound, this self would leap
To fullest life and be awake and whole.

"And He said unto all, If any man would come after Me, let him deny himself, and take up his cross daily, and follow Me" (*Luke* ix. 23).

By Reality we mean that all the hidden powers of our life are in perfect harmony with themselves and in perfect harmony with God. None of us are real in the full sense of the word; we become real bit by bit as we obey the Spirit of God. It is not a question of sham and reality or of hypocrisy and reality, but of sincerity being transformed into reality. It is possible to be perfectly real to ourselves but not real to God; that is not reality. It is possible to be perfectly real to ourselves and real to other people, but not real in our relationship to God; that is not reality. The only reality is being in harmony with ourselves and other people and God. That is the one great reality towards which God is working, and towards which we are working as we obey Him.

(1) SELF-REALIZATION—NATURALLY. "If any man would come after Me,"

It is a painful process becoming conscious of one's self; we are not conscious of ourselves at the beginning of life. A child has no realization of himself as distinct from those round about him, consequently he is in complete harmony. When a child begins to realize himself he becomes self-

32

conscious and his distress begins; he begins to find he is different from everyone else and thinks that no one understands him, and he becomes either conceited or depressed.

(a) *Sense of Individualism.* The critical moment in a man or woman's life is when they realize they are individually separate from other people. When I realize I am separate from everyone else, the danger is that I think I am different from everyone else. Immediately I think that, I become a law to myself; that means I excuse everything I do, but nothing anyone else does. 'My temptations are peculiar,' I say; 'my setting is very strange; no one knows but myself the peculiar forces that are in me.' When first that big sense awakens that I am different from everyone else, it is the seed of all lawlessness and all immoralities.

(b) *Sense of Intuition.* This sense that I know what other people do not know, that I have a special intuition that tells me things, is even more dangerous than the sense of individualism because it leads to spiritual deception in a religious nature and to hard intellectual conceit in a natural nature.

(c) *Sense of Isolation.* When a person realizes he is alone the danger of inordinate affection arises. Have you ever noticed the remarkable phrase in the Song of Songs— ". . . stir not up, nor awaken love, until it please"? The forces of the world, the flesh and the devil are set to do that one thing, to awaken the soul's love before the true Lover of the soul, the Lord Jesus Christ, has been revealed. It would serve us well if we thought a great deal more from the ethical side of our Christian work than we do. We think of it always from the spiritual side because that is the natural way for us, but when we think of it from the ethical side we get at it from a different angle. More damage is done because souls have been left alone on the moral side than Christian workers ever dream, simply because their eyes are blinded by seeing only along the spiritual line. When once the powers of a nature, young or old, begin to awaken it realizes that it is an individual; that it has a power of knowing without reasoning, and it

33

begins to be afraid because it is alone and looks for a companion, and the devil is there always to supply the need. Remember the old proverb—"If you knock long enough at a door the devil may open it." The Bible indicates that there is a wrong as well as a right perseverance.

Self-realization naturally means—I must develop my nature along its natural line: I am an individual, therefore I shall take care that no one who is not like me teaches me; I have gifts of soul that make me feel a strong affinity for certain natures, those I shall foster; I feel very much alone, therefore I shall select another person or persons to comrade me. The Spirit of God counteracts these tendencies of the nature which He has created until they flow into the right channels.

There are many signs of religiosity in a young life that arise simply from natural physical development and are not spiritual at all. A boy or girl in their teens often shows amazingly religious tendencies and these are mistaken for the real work of the Spirit of God; they may or may not be. The need for spiritual discernment on this point in those of us who are workers is intense. Whenever there is real spiritual life, Jesus Christ is in the first place; when it is not the work of the Spirit of God there are vague notions about God, aspirations after this and that, and great strivings that may end anywhere, towards God or not. The great need is for the Holy Spirit to introduce Jesus Christ. The supreme moment for Our Lord in any life is when that individual life is beginning to awaken. The incalculable power of intercession comes in here. A Christian father or mother or teacher or friend can anticipate that moment in the life of their child or teacher or friend, so that when the awakening comes, the Spirit of God in answer to believing prayer holds off the world, the flesh and the devil and introduces the Friend of friends, the Lord Jesus Christ. I wish I could convey to you the imperative importance of intercessory prayer. If the devil is anxious about one thing he is anxious not to allow us to see this; if we will only say, 'Well, prayer does not much matter; they are very young and inexperienced.' Forestall the time; hold off the devil! We do not know when a nature begins to awaken along the line of self-realization, it may be very early in life or later on; but I do believe that by intercessory prayer, as Jesus Himself has told us, the great power of God works in ways we cannot conceive. I think sometimes we will be covered with shame when we meet the Lord Jesus and think how blind and ignorant we were when He brought people around us to pray for, or gave us opportunities of warning, and instead of praying we tried to find out what was wrong. We have no business to try and find out what is wrong, our business is to pray, so that when the awakening comes Jesus Christ will be the first they meet. The one who meets a nature at its awakening has the opportunity of making or marring that life. As soon as Jesus Christ touches 'the chords of being,' the nature is fascinated by Him, as the early disciples were—no work of regeneration as yet, simply the holding of the nature entranced by Jesus Christ. The chances for the devil in that life are very poor indeed; but if the world, the flesh and the devil get the first touch, a long line of havoc may follow before Jesus Christ has His chance.

(2) CHRIST-REALIZATION. "let him deny himself,"

Jesus is talking to men who have reached the point of self-realization naturally; now He is requiring from them an identification with Himself.

"It is not only that they identify themselves in a fidelity which is indistinguishable from that which is due to God alone, but that He, in the most solemn, explicit, and overpowering words, requires from them that identification, and makes their eternal destiny depend upon it." (Denny.)

Self-realization naturally cares nothing about God, it does not care whether Jesus lived or died or did anything at all. For ourselves we live and for ourselves we die; that is self-realization that leads to death and despair; it is absolutely and radically opposed to Christ-realization. True self-realization is exhibited in the life of Our Lord, perfect

35

harmony with God and a perfect understanding of man; and He prays "that they may be one, even as We are one."

(*a*) *Power of Asceticism.* Asceticism is the passion of giving up things, and is recognizable in a life not born again of the Spirit of God. It is all very well if it ends in giving up the one thing God wants us to give up, viz. our right to ourselves, but if it does not end there, it will do endless damage to the life. In a sanctified soul the power of asceticism shows itself in an understanding of the mighty place of martyrdom in Our Lord's programme for a disciple. "Let him deny himself." These words of Jesus reveal the line He continually worked on when He talked to the disciples; He introduced the closest ties and said that at times even these have to be severed if we are to be true to Him. That sounds harsh to anyone if he has not come into the understanding of Jesus that we get after sanctification.

"Consider how great this Man is who declares that the final destiny of men depends on whether or not they are loyal to Him, and who demands absolute loyalty though it involve sacrifice of the tenderest affections, and the surrender of life in the most ignominious death." (*Denny.*)

(*b*) *Passion of Absorption.* When Jesus Christ is seen by a newly awakened nature His fascination is complete—no conviction of sin, no reception of the Holy Spirit, no believing even, but an absorbing passion for Jesus Christ. There are a great number of Christians in this immature stage, they write books and conduct meetings along the line of being absorbed in Jesus, but we have the feeling as we listen—'There is something lacking—what is it?' What is lacking is the realization that we have to be brought by means of the death of Jesus into the relationship to God that Our Lord Himself had. The hymns that are written by people in this stage emphasize the human aspect of Jesus, but there is no real gripping power in them for the saint.

The passion of absorption is also recognizable in the initial stages of sanctification, perhaps more so than at any other stage; there is no consciousness of a separate life.

To talk about suffering and cross-bearing and self-denial is not only outside the soul's vocabulary but outside the possibility of his thinking, he seems to be absolutely absorbed in Christ. This stage is excessively dangerous unless it leads to one thing, identification with the death of Jesus.

(c) *Perseverance of Adoration.* When Jesus touches a nature, a long series of devotional hours characterizes the life—always wanting times of being alone with God, always wanting to pray and read devotional books. In some natures it goes as far as ecstasy. After sanctification the characteristic of the life is clear—Jesus Christ first, Jesus Christ second and Jesus Christ third, all that the Lord wants; the life goes on with a flood of intense energy, adoration unspeakable. "I live," said Paul, "and yet no longer I, but Christ liveth in me." The identity is changed, the very faith, the very nature that was in Jesus is in us now, and we with all other saints may grow into the full realization of God's purpose in Redemption. ". . . till we all attain unto the unity of the faith." We cannot attain to it alone.

(3) SELF-REALIZATION—SPIRITUALLY. "and take up his cross daily, and follow Me."

In the first experience of sanctification we lose altogether the consciousness of our own identity, we are absorbed in God; but that is not the final place, it is merely the introduction to a totally new life. We lose our natural identity and consciously gain the identity that Jesus had, and it is when God begins to deal with sanctified souls on that line that darkness sometimes comes and the strange misunderstanding of God's ways. They are being taught what God taught Abraham:

> My goal is God Himself, not joy, nor peace,
> Nor even blessing, but Himself, my God.

Jesus said to His disciples, "I have yet many things to say unto you, but ye cannot bear them now." They could not bear them until the Holy Spirit brought them into the realization of Who Jesus was.

(a) *Patient Dedication.* "and take up his cross" The immature stage of the life of sanctification merges into a clear, patient dedication to Jesus Christ; free from all hurry spiritually and all panic there is a slow and growing realization of what Jesus meant when He said, "As the Father hath sent Me, even so am I sending you." Our cross is the steady exhibition of the fact that we are not our own but Christ's, and we know it, and are determined to be unenticed from living a life of dedication to Him. This is the beginning of the emergence of the real life of faith.

(b) *Plain Daylight.* "daily," The life of manifestations is a critical stage in the saint's experience. The real life of the saint on this earth, and the life that is most glorifying to Jesus, is the life that steadfastly goes on through common days and common ways, with no mountain-top experiences. We read that John the Baptist "looked upon Jesus *as He walked* . . ."—not at Jesus in a prayer meeting or in a revival service, or Jesus performing miracles; he did not watch Him on the Mount of Transfiguration, he did not see Him in any great moment at all, he saw Him on an ordinary day when Jesus was walking in an ordinary common way, and he said, "Behold, the Lamb of God!" That is the test of reality. Mounting up with wings as eagles, running and not being weary, are indications that something more than usual is at work. Walking and not fainting is the life that glorifies God and satisfies the heart of Jesus to the full—the plain daylight life, unmarked, unknown, only occasionally, if ever, does the marvel of it break on other people.

(c) *Persistent Devotion.* "and follow Me." This is the life of martyrdom with the glowing heat of perfect love at its heart. Only one Figure ahead and that the Lord Jesus, other people, saints or sinners, shadows. The mark of this life of devotion is its persistence. Spasms are a sign of returning or departing life. The continual feeling, 'I must wind myself up, I have been letting things go, I must screw my life up and get to work,' may be a sign that we are coming nearer the source of the true life or it may be exactly the opposite, it may be a sign that we are declining into death. God and ourselves are the only judges of that. The one thing to fix on is that the life Jesus lived is the pattern of what our lives will be when once we come to the place of self-realization spiritually.

"No one is worthy of Jesus who does not follow Him, as it were, with the rope round his neck—ready to die the most ignominious death rather than prove untrue." (Denny.)

The idea of martyrdom is the very essence of the saint's life. Jesus Christ always used the figure of martyrdom when He spoke of this stage of the Christian life (*see* John xxi. 18). The saint at this stage is leagues beyond the point of asking—'Am I doing God's will?' he *is* God's will; leagues beyond the point of saying—'I do want God to bless me here and use me there'; leagues beyond the point of saying—'I have got the victory' and praising God for it; he is in the place where God can make him broken bread and poured-out wine just as He made His Son broken bread and poured-out wine for us.

May this message make clear to our hearts and minds the purpose of God in our salvation and sanctification. God's purpose is to make us real, that is, to make us perfectly at one with all our own powers and perfectly at one with God, no longer children but understanding in our heads as well as in our hearts the meaning of the Redemption, and slowly maturing until we are a recommendation to the redeeming grace of our Lord Jesus Christ. As the angels look down on us, do they see something that makes them marvel at the wonderful workmanship of Jesus Christ— "When He shall come to be glorified in His saints, and to be marvelled at in all them that believed"?

JUDGMENT

Oh, we're sunk enough here, God knows!
 But not quite so sunk that moments,
Sure tho' seldom, are denied us,
 When the spirit's true endowments
Stand out plainly from its false ones,
 And apprise it if pursuing
Or the right way or the wrong way,
 To its triumph or undoing.

R. B.

"And this is the judgement, that the light is come into the world, and men loved the darkness rather than the light; for their works were evil" (*John* iii. 19, R.V.).

The healthiest exercise for the mind of a Christian is to learn to apprehend the truth granted to it in vision. Every Christian with any experience at all has had a vision of some fundamental truth, either about the Atonement or the Holy Spirit or sin, and it is at the peril of their souls that they lose the vision. By prayer and determination we have to form the habit of keeping ourselves soaked in the vision God has given. The difficulty with the majority of us is that we will not seek to apprehend the vision, we get glimpses of it and then leave it alone. "I was not disobedient to the heavenly vision," says Paul. It is one of the saddest things to see men and women who have had visions of truth but have failed to apprehend them, and it is on this line that judgment comes. It is not a question of intellectual discernment or of knowing how to present the vision to others, but of seeking to apprehend the vision so that it may apprehend us. Soak and soak and soak continually in the one great truth of which you have had a vision; take it to bed with you, sleep with it, rise up in the morning with it, continually bring your imagination into captivity to it, and slowly and surely as the months and years go by God will make you one of His specialists in that particular truth. God is no respecter of persons.

(1) THE MASTER MEANING OF CRISIS. "And this is the judgment," i.e. the critical moment.

A man is not judged by his ordinary days and nights because in these he is more or less a creature of drift, but a crisis is immediately his test. A crisis is a turning-point that separates, and it will always reveal character. If, after a crisis is passed, you will take the trouble to go back, you will find there was a moment away back when a clear idea was given you of what God wanted you to do and you did not do it; the days have gone on and suddenly the crisis comes, and instantly judgment is passed. The thing that tells is the crisis. The generality of men drift along without bothering their heads about anything until a crisis comes, and it is always critical.

(a) *The Critical Issue.* Mark vi. 16: "But Herod, when he heard thereof, said, John, whom I beheaded, he is risen." The crisis in the case of Herod was brought about by the disciples' preaching of Jesus; when "His name had become known," Herod was mastered and made known to himself; the crisis revealed a terror-stricken conscience. Herod was a Sadducee and "the Sadducees say that there is no resurrection," but when the name of Jesus was noised abroad, he was superstitiously terrified and said, "John, whom I beheaded, he is risen."

(b) *The Convicting Idea.* Mark vi. 18: "For John said unto Herod, It is not lawful for thee to have thy brother's wife." The convicting idea was produced by what Herod heard; the truth had been spoken to him, he had been convicted by it—"he heard him gladly," and "did many things" (v. 20, R.V. marg.), but not the one thing. Herod refused to obey the light when it was given, and it was that moment that determined how he would show himself in the crisis.

(c) *The Confirming Intention.* Mark vi. 21: "And when a convenient day was come . . ." The convenient day will always come, the convenient day for the satisfaction of sin. This is a general principle which the generality of Christian workers do not seem to realize. Sin has got to be

41

satisfied, or else strangled to death by a supernatural power. Hell is the satisfaction of all sin. Sentimentalism arises in the nature that is unused to facing realities. People will pile on Christian work, will do anything, will slave to further orders, rather than let you touch the thing that is wrong. Great oceans of penitence and confession are shown, but when all that is through you find there is one fact more, one blind spot which the one you are dealing with refuses to look at or to let you look at. If you are a servant of God, you must ruthlessly rip up the sentimental humbug and go direct to the one thing.

These three things play their part in every crisis. Be careful to note, however, that a crisis does not make character; a crisis reveals character. No sane person is allowed by God to live continually in the light of his conscience. The characteristic of the life of a saint is essential elemental simplicity. Apart from moments of crisis, character is not consciously known. You can see this every day you live; we all say—'If I had been in your place, I should have done so and so.' You have no means of knowing what you would have done; the nature of a crisis is that it takes you unawares, it happens suddenly, and the line you take reveals your character; it may also reveal something that amazes you. For instance, you may think a certain person selfish, self-interested and self-satisfied, but a crisis comes, bereavement or a business disaster or sickness, and to your amazement you find he or she is not the self-interested person you thought they were at all, there are whole tracts of generosity in their nature of which you knew nothing. Or you may think a person very generous and kind and loving, and when a crisis occurs, to your amazement and every one else's, they show themselves mean and selfish and cruel. The crisis is always the judgment.

(2) THE MORAL MAJESTY OF THE CRITERION. "That the light is come into the world."

What does Jesus Christ say the standard of God's judgment is for us all? The Light that has come into the world.

Who is the Light of the world? The Lord Jesus Christ, Son of God and Son of Man.

"To judge is to see clearly, to care for what is just, and therefore to be impartial and impersonal." (*Amiel.*)

A few moments' consideration will reveal what a difficult task the Holy Spirit has in bringing even the best of saints to this impersonal standard of judgment. This idea, which shows our personal way of looking at things, is always lurking about us—'Oh well, God knows I really meant to devote myself to Him and to obey Him, but so many things have upset me; I have not had the opportunities I should have had.' 'I don't really mean to speak and act as I do, but I shall not count it this time.' All this shows how difficult it is for the Holy Spirit to bring us to apply the standard of Jesus Christ to ourselves, we will apply His standard to other people; but Jesus Christ brings it home to us. Am I willing to obey the light? We have to beware of personal interests which blur the mind from accepting Our Lord's standard. To walk in the light, as God is in the light, is the one condition of being kept cleansed from all sin.

(*a*) *The Standard for the Heathen.* John 1. 9; Rom. ii. 11–16; Matt. xxv. 31–46.

The first thing to ask in regard to this standard is—what about the people who have never heard of Jesus Christ, and may never hear of Him, how are they judged? The passages given all refer to God's standard of judgment for the heathen, viz. the light they have, not the light they have never had and could not get. Conscience is the standard by which men and women are to be judged until they have been brought into contact with the Lord Jesus Christ. The call to preach the Gospel to the heathen is not the frenzied doctrine that the heathen who have never known Jesus Christ, and never had the chance of knowing Him, are going to be eternally lost, but the command of Jesus Christ—"Go ye into all the world, and preach the gospel to every creature."

(*b*) *The Standard for Christendom.* John iii. 18: "He that believeth on Him is not judged: he that believeth not hath been judged already, because he hath not believed on the

43

name of the only begotten Son of God." The standard for the judgment of Christendom is not the light it has received but the light it ought to have received. Every country in Christendom has had plenty of opportunity of knowing about Christ, and the doom of a soul begins the moment it consciously neglects to know Jesus Christ or consciously rejects Him when He is known. Beware of applying Our Lord's words in Matthew xxv. to Christians; Matthew xxv. is not the standard for the judgment of Christians, but the standard for the judgment of the nations that do not know Christ. The standard for the judgment of Christians is Our Lord.

(c) *The Standard for the Church.* Eph. iv. 11-13: "And He gave some to be apostles; and some, prophets; and some, evangelists; and some, pastors and teachers; . . . till we all attain unto the unity of the faith." These verses do not refer to individual Christian lives but to the collective life of the saints. The individual saint cannot be perfected apart from others. "He gave some to be apostles . . .," for what purpose? To show how clever they were, what gifts they had? No, "for the perfecting of the saints." In looking back over the history of the Church we find that every one of these 'gifts' has been tackled. Paul says that apostles, prophets, evangelists, pastors and teachers, are all meant for one thing by God, viz. "for the perfecting of the saints, . . . unto the building up of the body of Christ." No saint can ever be perfected in isolation or in any other way than God has laid down. There are very few who are willing to apprehend that for which they were apprehended, they thank God for salvation and sanctification and then stagnate, consequently the perfecting of the saints is hindered.

(3) THE MAKING MOMENT OF CHOICE. " And men loved the darkness rather than the light; for their works were evil."

Our choice is indelibly marked for time and eternity. What we decide makes our destiny, not what we have felt, nor what we have been moved to do, or inspired to see, but what we decide to do in a given crisis, it is that which makes or mars us. Sooner or later there comes to every life the question—Will I choose to side with God's verdict on sin in the Cross of Christ? I may say 'I won't accept,' or 'I will put it off,' but both are decisions, remember.

(a) *The Prejudice for Darkness*. Matt. vi. 23: "If therefore the light that is in thee be darkness, how great is that darkness!" The disposition of a man determines the way he will decide when the crisis comes, but the only One Who knows the disposition other than the man himself is God. The unaltered, natural disposition of a man is called by our Lord 'darkness,' that means prejudice against the light.

(b) *The Persistence of Direction*. Mark vi. 26–27: "And the king was exceeding sorry; but for the sake of his oaths, and of them that sat at meat, he would not reject her. And straightway the king sent forth a soldier of his guard, and commanded to bring his head. . . ." John the Baptist represented the voice of God to Herod; Herod decided to silence the voice of God. He had one subsequent twinge (*see* Mark vi. 16–18); then his conscience never bothered him again, and Jesus Christ and all He represented became a farce to him. We read in Luke xxiii. 8–9, that "when Herod saw Jesus, he was exceeding glad: for he was of a long time desirous to see Him; and he hoped to see some miracle done by Him. And he questioned Him in many words; but He answered him nothing." Herod had ordered the voice of God to be silent, and it was; and now all sails are set for perdition. His was "a ghastly smooth life, dead at heart." That is the awful condition to which a man may get where he no longer believes in goodness or purity or justice; but the Bible never allows that a man can get there without being culpable in God's sight. Whenever you see a soul in danger of closing over one sin, go at it no matter how it hurts or how annoyed that soul is with you, go at it until the sin is blasted right out, never palliate it or sympathize. Very few voices rise up against the sins that make for the seal of silence on men and women and churches. This is what is lacking to-day.

(c) *Pronouncement of Destiny*. Luke xxiii. 9: "And he questioned Him in many words; but He answered him nothing." The reason "He answered him nothing" is to be found in Mark vi. 26–7. Herod decided to silence the voice of God in his life, and when the Son of God stood before him, he saw nothing in Him; there was no more compunction of conscience. Whenever a man makes the decision that Herod made—'I don't want to hear any more about the matter,' it is the beginning of the silence of God in his soul. To silence the voice of God is damnation in time; eternal damnation is that for ever. "God answereth me no more" (1 Sam. xxviii. 15) is an expression of damnation in time. Divine silence is the ultimate destiny of the man who refuses to come to the light and obey it.

It is a terrible thing in the spiritual career not to be apprehended by the light that has been given; it may have been at some midday or midnight; in childhood or in the early days of your Christian life, or as recently as last week, you know exactly when it was, it is between you and God, are you going to decide along that line—'My God, I don't know all that it means, but I decide for it'? Whenever any light is given you on any fundamental issue and you refuse to settle your soul on it and apprehend it, your doom is sealed along that particular line. If when a clear emphatic vision of some truth is given you by God, not to your intellect but to your heart, and in spite of it all you decide to take another course, the vision will fade and may never come back.

There are men and women who ought to be princes and princesses with God but they are away on God's left, they may even be sanctified, but they are left at a particular stage because they chose to be left; instead of obeying the heavenly vision, the natural judicious decisions of an average Christian life have been preferred. It has nothing to do with salvation, but with lost opportunities in service for God. "Many are called, but few chosen," i.e. few prove themselves the chosen ones. Whenever the vision comes, let me plead with you, as though God were intreating by me, do not be disobedient to it, because there is only one purpose in our lives, and that is the satisfaction of the Lord Jesus Christ.

BACKSLIDING

John vi

The tendencies that make temptation possible are inherent in man as God created him, Adam and Our Lord Jesus Christ being witnesses; and we have to bear in mind that regeneration does not remove those tendencies but rather increases them. The possibility of temptation reaches its height in Jesus Christ.

(1) TENDENCY TO REPOSE. "It takes so much effort to maintain one's self in an exceptional point of view that one falls back into prejudice by pure exhaustion."

The tendency to repose physically is a right law of our physical nature; morally and spiritually it is a tendency towards immorality and unspirituality.

(a) *The Desire for Rest—The Arrest of Desire.* vv. 10–15. The desire at the heart of true spiritual life is for union with God; the tendency to rest in anything less than the realization of this desire becomes the arrest of desire. Whenever we seek repose in any blessing spiritually, sleeping sickness begins. The tendency to rest in any of the blessings which are the natural outcome of union with God is the beginning of backsliding. Is my desire for union with God, or am I like the people who sought to make Jesus King—for what purpose? If Jesus could feed their bodies without their having to work, that was the very thing they wanted. The incident is symbolic of the tendency to repose which is inherent in human nature, but if this desire were satisfied it would be the destruction of all character.

(b) *The Decay of Reality—The Dawn of Death.* vv. 30–1. Reality means that which is in perfect accord with God. If I accept any blessing of God, e.g. sanctification, as the final end and aim of my life, from that moment decay begins in my spiritual life. Sanctification is the gateway to real union with God, which is life unutterable. Peter points out this very thing in his Epistles; he says, you know these things and are established in the truth, but you are going to sleep, you are in danger of mistaking this for the final place; it is not, it is only the introduction. (2 Peter i. 12–13.) Are we sufficiently well taught of the Holy Spirit to stir up souls who have got right with God, until they come to the reality of realities, absolute oneness with God?

The tendency to backslide begins right in the very secret places. No wonder Jesus urged His disciples to watch and pray, "that ye enter not into temptation." The possibility of backsliding is so full of peril that the only safety is to look to Jesus, relying on the Holy Spirit, and never to allow the repose which is a necessity physically to come into the life of the spirit. The arrest of desire begins when I want to rest in spiritual blessings; and the dawn of death in spiritual life begins when I become smugly satisfied with my attainments—'This is all God wants of me.' What God wants of me is all that He has revealed in Jesus Christ. "till we all attain unto the measure of the stature of the fullness of Christ" (Eph. iv. 13). The rest which is the outcome of entire sanctification is not the rest of stagnation, but the rest of the reality of union with God.

(c) *The Dreams of Repose—The Night of Disaster. vv. 34-5.* These words of Our Lord are a puzzle to an unspiritual mind, and an unspiritual mind is produced by allowing visions and dreams of spiritual repose which Jesus Christ continually discourages. What do I dream about and allow my mind to fancy when in communion with God? One of the greatest snares in spiritual life is to foster dreams and fancies of our own which do not tally with the statements of Jesus, instead of bringing every thought into captivity to the obedience of Christ. People who go off at a tangent and are led astray by Satan as an angel of light are deceived just here. Disaster spiritually follows whenever the tendency to repose is yielded to. "Forgetting the things which are behind, and stretching forward to the things which are before . . ." is the only attitude for a saint.

(2) THE TENDENCY TO REVERT. "Is not life the test of
our moral force, and all these untold waverings are they
not temptations of the soul?"

In all organic life there is a tendency to revert to the
original type. Flowers and plants may be highly developed
and cultivated, but if afterwards they are left alone year
after year they will revert to the original type from which
they sprang. The spiritual application of this is that there
is the possibility in every child of God of reverting to the
original type of self-interest; but thank God there is also
the possibility of being transformed into the image of God's
Son (Rom. viii. 29).

(a) *Possibility of Offence.* *v.* 52. The possibility of offence
can only come when two persons have somewhat the same
nature. People who have no affinity with Jesus run no risk
of being offended with Him; but no Christian is ever free
from that possibility (cf. Matt. xi. 6). Satan comes to us
with suggestions—'Surely God would never ask you to do
such and such a thing? God would never guide you in such
a way?' But God does. The possibility of offence is there
immediately I become a child of God.

(b) *The Perversity of the Offended.* *vv.* 60–1. Perversity
means to turn away from one to whom I have been devoted
because he says things that do not suit my ideas. There is
a stage in spiritual experience, it may be before or after
sanctification, when this perversity is possible. Someone
comes with an exposition of a truth of God I have never
realized before and at once the possibility of perversity is
awakened and I say, 'No, I am sure God would never have
revealed this truth to you if He has not revealed it to me.'
The possibility of offence is always there, and perversity
is the next step. As soon as I am offended I become perverse, my eyes are blinded and I see only along the line of
my prejudices. There are saints, for instance, who reso-
lutely shut their minds against the truth that they can draw
upon the Lord's life for their bodies, or against the need
for being continually renewed in their minds. This will

lead not only to stagnation spiritually but to perversity. The only safety is to keep in the light as God is in the light.

(c) *The Perfidy of the Offended.* v. 66. "Upon this many of His disciples went back, and walked no more with Him." Reversion to self-will, and insisting on my own way of serving God, is not only utter faithlessness to Jesus Christ, but active working against the particular truth which has offended me. The people who are most perverse against the truth are those who know it. This is stated in its most extreme form in Hebrews vi. 4–6.

If God were to remove from us as saints the possibility of disobedience there would be no value in our obedience, it would be a mechanical business. To say after sanctification, 'Now I can do what I like,' is a perilously dangerous statement. If it were true, it would never have been recorded that "even Christ pleased not Himself." The possibility of disobedience in a child of God makes his obedience of amazing value. The one who is not a child of God is the slave of the wrong disposition, he has not the power to obey; immediately God delivers him from the wrong disposition, he is free to obey, and consequently free to disobey, and it is this that makes temptation possible. Temptation is not sin; temptation must always be possible for our sonship to be of worth to God. It would be no credit for God to bring mechanical slaves to glory—"for it became Him . . . in bringing many *sons* unto glory"—not slaves, not useless channels, but vigorous, alert, wide-awake men and women, with all their powers and faculties devoted absolutely to God.

(3) TENDENCY TO REVOLT. "The independence which is the condition of individuality is at the same time the eternal temptation of the individual."

Spiritual revolt means the deliberately forsaking of God and signing on under another ruler. We must distinguish between degeneration and revolt. We have been dealing with the tendencies that lead to degeneration, no positive side has been taken yet, but there is a distinct disinclination to go on further—'I am thankful I am here, and here I am going to stay'—without realizing that we cannot stay where we are, we must either go on or go back—and that leads ultimately to revolt, not mere declension but a deliberate signing on under another ruler. "For My people have committed two evils; they have forsaken Me the fountain of living waters"—that is not backsliding; that is degeneration; "and have hewed them out cisterns, broken cisterns, that can hold no water"—these two things together constitute backsliding. The words God uses in connection with backsliding are terrible. He uses words that shock us as moral individuals in order to portray what backsliding is in His sight (e.g. Jer. iii. 8).

(a) *The Reaction of the Unattained. vv.* 41, 52. When a soul realizes the truth of God and fails to attain it, there lies within him a power of reaction which not only means he will try no more but he will dissuade others. If once we have had a vision from God of His purpose for us and we leave it unattained, the tendency is to say, 'Oh well, it may be meant for other people, but it isn't for me.' This tendency is in every one of us, we scarcely discern it, but it is there. For anyone to leave unattained anything Our Lord has revealed as possible for him, is the beginning of Satan's chance over that soul. Our Lord makes no allowance for not attaining because by means of His Cross we have all the marvellous grace of God to draw upon, all the mighty life of the Lord Jesus Christ to enable us to attain. A great many of us try and attain without having received the life of Jesus and we are bound to fail; that is not a matter of reaction, it is inevitable. But if we have received the life of Jesus, it is unconscious blasphemy in God's sight to stop short of attaining anything He reveals as possible for us. Our Lord's illustration of salt that has lost its savour is applicable. "Ye are the salt of the earth: but if the salt have lost its savour, wherewith shall it be salted? It is thenceforth good for nothing, but to be cast out and trodden under foot of men." Savourless salt is a most cursed influence in the physical world, and a saint who has lost his saintliness is a pestilential influence in the spiritual world. We lose saintliness whenever we take our eyes for one second off the Source of our life, the Lord Jesus Christ. Whenever we do, all these errors begin to be possible. But if we keep in the light with God our life is that of a child, simple and joyful all through. It is sufficient for a child to know that his father wishes him to do certain things and he learns to draw on a strength greater than his own and attains and attains; if he does not, he runs the risk of becoming a prodigal.

(b) *The Reviling of the Unreached. v.* 61. If a man has really tasted the life of God and knows God's purpose for him, or did know it months or years ago, but has never fulfilled that purpose through obedience, the tendency to revile the standard is irresistible. We must revile a standard we have not reached when we know we ought to have reached it. It is not something that can be prevented, it is inevitable. If once we deliberately stop short and refuse to let God's life have its way with us, we shall revile the truth because it has not been reached.

There are two things which keep us from going on with God—first, the 'show business'; by the 'show business' we mean the desire to appeal to the largest number: if you do that, you will have to lower the standards of Jesus Christ ; and second, sympathy. Sympathy with one another that does not spring from sympathy with God's interests in that one will always end in reviling some standard of God's truth. It will not mean you use reviling language, you may use very pious and sighing language—'Oh no, *I* could never attain to that.' You may preach entire sanctification and your message may be couched in beautiful language, then you say—'This is God's standard, but of course I am not there. There can be only one result in the souls of those who listen, and that is the reviling of the standard, for which you and I will be called to account. The glibness and ease with which men proclaim the great standards of Jesus Christ and then sweep them away by saying, 'God forbid I should say I am there,' makes one tremble, because such a statement implies, Jesus Christ cannot bring me there, it is an ideal to which I cannot attain. When we come to the New Testament there is the quiet and grandly-easy certainty that we *can* attain. All God's commands are enablings. Never sympathize with a soul who cannot get through to God on Jesus Christ's lines. The Lord is never hard nor cruel, He is the essence of tender compassion and gentleness. The reason any soul cannot get through is that there is something in him that won't budge; immediately it does, Jesus Christ's marvellous life will have its way.

(c) *The Renunciation by Unbelief.* vv. 70–1. Not only is it possible for a soul to revile the standards set up by Jesus, but it is possible to do what Judas did, renounce Him by unbelief. It is easy to make Judas the arch-sinner, but he is the type of what is possible in every one of us. Thank God that the Apostle Paul is also a possible type for everyone of us, but do not forget that Judas is a possible type too.

These are terrible truths, but it is the terrors of the dark night which drive us closer to the haven of unutterable security, the Lord Jesus Christ. No wonder God's Book says, "the way of transgressors is hard." Could God have made it more terrible than He has for man to go astray? Could He have put the danger signals more clearly than He has? The way is absolutely strewn with alarm signals; it is impossible to go wrong easily.

Thus in new ways we learn the profound beauty of Our Lord's words: "Come unto Me"; "*I* am the Way, the Truth and the Life."

TEMPTATION

1 *Cor*. x. 12–13.

The word "temptation" has come down in the world, we use it wrongly nowadays. Temptation is not sin, it is the thing we are bound to meet if we are men; not to be tempted would be to be beneath contempt. Temptation is something that exactly fits the nature of the one tempted, and is therefore a great revealer of the possibilities of the nature. Every man has the setting of his own temptation. A good illustration of temptation is the way steel is tested. Steel can be 'tired' in the process of testing, and in this way its strength is measured. Temptation means the test by an alien power of the possessions held by a personality. This makes the temptation of Our Lord explainable: He held in His Person the fact that He was to be the King of men and the Saviour of the world, and the alien power that came to test Him on these lines is called in the Bible, Satan.

Temptation is also a severe test to fulfil the possessions of personality by a short cut. Temptation trains innocence into character or else into corruption. There are some temptations, however, by which we have no business to be tempted any longer; we should be on a higher plane dealing with other temptations. We may have our morality well within our own grasp and be comparatively free from temptation, but as soon as we are regenerated by the Spirit of God we begin to understand the force of spiritual temptations of which we were unconscious before.

(1) TEMPTATION *v.* SIN. *Jas*. i. 12–15.

Temptation and sin are profoundly different. Temptation is a pathway to the end desired, but it leads to a perplexing situation, inasmuch as it makes a man decide which factor he will obey in the dilemma. The possibility of sin and the inclination to sin are different things. Every man has the possibility of committing murder, but the inclination is not there. The inclination is as the deed, whether it is carried out or not (Rom. ii. 1; 1 John iii. 15). Satan had the possibility of disobedience and when the temptation producing the dilemma came, he inclined to rebellion against God. Adam had the possibility of disobedience, and when temptation came to him producing the dilemma, he deliberately inclined to disobedience, and the disposition to disobey God became the inheritance of the whole of the human race. "Wherefore, as by one man sin entered into the world, and death by sin; and so death passed upon all men, for that all have sinned" (Rom. v. 12). The disposition of sin is fundamental anarchy against God's rule over me, and as long as that disposition remains, temptation finds an inclination to sin in me; but when Our Lord delivers me from the disposition of sin, the hour of temptation discovers no inclination to sin, it tests the door of possibility only. "But now being made free from sin, and become servants to God, ye have your fruit unto holiness, and the end everlasting life" (Rom. vi. 22). Our Lord Jesus Christ had the possibility of disobedience, but when the temptation producing the dilemma came to Him, it found no inclination to disobedience; and everyone that is saved by Him is put in the position He was in when He was tempted (see Heb. ii. 11; iv. 15–16). Until a man is regenerated and sanctified the general character of Our Lord's temptation is unguessed.

The sinless perfection heresy arises out of this confusion—it says that because the disposition of sin is removed, it is impossible to sin. The inclination to sin, thank God, is removed, but never the possibility. If the power to disobey were removed, our obedience would be of no value, for we should cease to be morally responsible. It is gloriously possible not to sin, but never impossible to sin, because we are moral agents. Morality must be militant in this order of things, but we can be 'more than conquerors' every time.

The temptation James speaks of is the temptation we know naturally—"Every man is tempted when he is drawn away by his own lust and enticed." Until we are born again we only understand this kind of temptation, but by regeneration we are lifted into another realm and have other temptations to face, viz. the kind of temptations Our Lord faced. The temptations of Jesus have no home at all in our natural human nature, they do not appeal to us. A man's disposition on the inside, i.e. what he possesses in his personality, determines by what he is tempted on the outside, and the temptation will always come along the line of the ruling disposition. Sin is a disposition of self-love that obeys every temptation to its own lordship. Sin is literally self-centred rule, a disposition that rules the life apart from God.

Naturally we are taught by this disposition to lust for what we desire, and lust will warp character from rectitude to ruin—"drawn away of his own lust, and enticed." The destiny of lust is peculiarly fascinating. It presents a wild reach of possibility, and lust stampedes when it is not constrained by the consideration that it will lead the character to infamy, not fame. Lust means 'I must have it at once, I will have my desire satisfied, and will brook no restraint.' Temptation yielded to is the birth of sin in the personal life and ends in death. The verses in James i. are the natural history of temptation. Lust is used in other ways in the Bible than merely of immorality, it is the spirit of 'I must have it at once,' no matter what it is. Temptation yielded to is lust deified.

The period of temptation in Our Lord's life came immediately after a time of spiritual exaltation (see Matt. iii. 16–17; iv. 1); it was a period of estimating forces, and the historic temptations of Jesus Christ are pictorial records of wrong ways to the kingdoms of God. At His Baptism Jesus Christ accepted the vocation of bearing away the sin of the world, and immediately He was put by God's Spirit into the testing machine of the devil. But He did not 'tire'; He went through the temptations 'without sin' and retained the possessions of His personality intact.

"Then the devil leaveth Him, and behold angels came and ministered unto Him" (Matt. iv. 11). The sign that you have gone through temptation rightly is that you retain your affinity with the highest.

(2) TEMPTATION AND JESUS CHRIST. *Matt*. iv. 1, 11; *Heb*. ii. 18; iv. 15–16.

External circumstances are made to form an exact counterpart of the internal desire, which is different in different men. For example, the temptation of Our Lord was quite different from the temptation of Judas Iscariot, because the inner disposition was different. We have to beware of saying that because Jesus was Divine, temptation to Him was not real. If that is so, then the record in the Bible of Our Lord's temptations is a mere farce and is misleading, and the writer to the Hebrews is untrue when he says of Jesus, "tempted—*yet without sin*."

Could Jesus Christ be tempted? Undoubtedly He could, because temptation and sin are not the same thing. The temptation James speaks of, and the temptation of Jesus, are very different in character. The temptations which beset us as ordinary men gather round the disposition of sin.

In Luke iii. 23 we read ". . . and Jesus Himself began to be about thirty years of age." That is the time in human life when man reaches maturity and all his powers are perfected; the time when he is spared no requirement of his manhood. Up to that time, life is full of promise, after that it is a matter of testing and attainment. After the baptism of Jesus and the descent of the Holy Ghost upon Him, God, as it were, took His sheltering hand off Him and let the devil do his worst.

Our Lord's temptation and ours move in different spheres until we are born again and become His brethren (Heb. ii. 11). The records of the temptation of Jesus are the records of how God as man is tempted, not of how man is tempted as man. The temptations of Jesus are not those of a man as man, but the temptation of GOD as man. Jesus Christ was not born with an heredity of sin. "Wherefore, it behoved Him in all things to be made like unto His brethren." His "brethren" are those in whom He is born. It is nowhere

57

said that Jesus Christ was 'tempted like as we are' as ordinary human beings. By regeneration the Son of God is formed in us, and He has the same setting in our physical life as He had when He was on earth. Are we remaining loyal to Him in the things which beset His life in us? The devil does not need to bother about the majority of us; we have enough lust on the inside to keep us in sin, but when once a man is born from above, the temptations alter instantly, and he realizes where the temptation is aimed, viz. at the disposition.

Our Lord was tested for the fulfilment of what He held in His own personal life, viz. the Saviourhood of the world and the Kingship of men, and the temptation by Satan was that He should fulfil these by a short cut. Our Lord's temptations were set by His disposition; He could not be tempted by lust, but He was tempted to the fulfilment of His incarnation along a line other than that marked out by His Father. Satan came to Him as an "angel of light," and the central citadel of the temptations was—'You are the Son of God, then do God's work in Your own way.' And at the heart of every one of Our Lord's answers is this— "I came to do My Father's work in His way, not in My own way" (see John vi. 38). Satan was right every time in his promise of what would happen if Our Lord took his suggested short cuts (see John vi. 15); but Our Lord would not be King of men on that line. He deliberately chose the "long, long trail," evading none of the suffering involved (see Heb. ii. 9–10).

(3) TEMPTATION, THE SINNER AND THE SAINT.

Matt. xxvi. 41; *Jas.* i. 14–15; *Luke* xxii. 28.

We all of us suffer from temptations we have no business to be suffering from, simply because we refuse to let God lift us to a higher plane where we would have other temptations to face of another type. The temptations of Jesus are removed from any affinity with the natural; but when we are born again we realize the meaning of Our Lord's words to Peter, "Satan hath desired to have you that he may sift you as wheat."

In our natural life we possess the possibility of self-realization—"I am going to get the best out of myself, and train myself for my own ends." Until we are born from above the highest standpoint we have is that of self-realization, and the particular possessions of our personality will be tested by the alien power to see whether that power can 'tire' it. Temptation is not towards what we understand as evil, but towards what we understand as good (cf. Luke xvi. 15). Temptation is something that for a while completely baffles us, we do not know whether it is towards a right thing or not.

Spiritual life is attained, not by a necromantic magic pill, but by moral choices, whereby we test the thing that presents itself to us as being good. The basis of natural life and moral and spiritual life is the same. The way we maintain health in each of these domains is by fight. Health is the balance between my physical life and external nature. If the fighting force on the inside begins to dwindle or is impaired, I get diseased, things outside begin to disintegrate my vital force. The same is true of my moral life, everything that does not partake of the nature of virtue is the enemy of virtue in me, and it depends on how much moral calibre I have whether I overcome and produce virtue. The same is true spiritually; if I have enough spiritual fighting capacity, I will produce a character like Jesus Christ's. Character must be attained, it is never given to us.

The devil does not tempt to wrong things, he tries to make us lose what God has put into us by regeneration, viz. the possibility of being of value to God. The central citadel of the devil's attack on Jesus Christ is the same in us when we are born from above, viz. my right to myself. Satan's aim is to dethrone God, and his whole purpose through the disposition of sin is to get us to the same place. Satan is never represented in the Bible as being guilty of sins, of doing wrong things; he is *a wrong being*.

There is a limit to temptation. "God is faithful who will

not suffer you to be tempted above that ye are able." God does not save us from temptations, but He succours us in the middle of them. In Hebrews iv. 15 the writer is not referring to the temptations common to man as fallen man, but to the temptations common to the sanctified soul. And when Our Lord taught His disciples to pray, "Lead us not into temptation," He is not referring to the temptation James refers to, but to the temptation He Himself was led into by the Spirit of God. After the baptism of Jesus and the descent of the Holy Ghost upon Him, God, as it were, took His sheltering hand off Him. So also after the work of sanctification, when the life of the saint really begins, God lifts His hand off us and lets the world do its worst, for He is assured that "He that is in him is greater than he that is against him."

CONSCIENCE

Conscience is that innate faculty in a man's spirit that attaches itself to the highest the man knows, whether he be an atheist or a Christian. The highest the Christian knows is God: the highest the atheist knows is his principles. That "Conscience is the voice of God" is easily proved to be absurd. If conscience were the voice of God, it would be the same in everyone. "I verily thought with myself," said Paul, "that I ought to do many things contrary to the name of Jesus of Nazareth" (Acts xxvi. 9). Paul acted according to his conscience; and Our Lord said, "Whosoever killeth you will think that he doeth God service" (John xvi. 2)—they will obey their conscience in putting you to death.

The eye in the body records exactly what it looks at. The eye simply records, and the record is according to the light thrown on what it looks at. Conscience is the eye of the soul which looks out on what it is taught is God, and how conscience records depends entirely upon what light is thrown upon God. Our Lord Jesus Christ is the only true light on God. When a man sees Jesus Christ he does not get a new conscience, but a totally new light is thrown upon God, and conscience records accordingly, with the result that he is absolutely upset by conviction of sin.

(1) THE ARTICLES OF CONSCIENCE.

By the 'articles' of conscience we mean the regulations of conscience in man fresh from the hand of his Creator, and those articles are—God is Love; God is Holy; God is Near. The Bible records that "God is love"; but it must be borne in mind that it is *the love of God*, and that love, which is inexpressible bliss to a Being like Jesus Christ, or to a being like Adam as God created him, is a veritable hell of pain to those of us who are not like either. To know that God is love, God is holy, God is near, is pure delight to man in his innocent relationship to God, but a terror extreme since the fall. God can never leave a man until He has burned him as pure as He is Himself. It is God's love that forbids He should let him go.

These regulations of conscience are ingrained in the spirit of fallen man as they are in the spirit of a man who is born from above.

(2) THE ATTITUDES OF CONSCIENCE.

When God is revealed as Love, as Holy, and as Near, it is man's conscience that alarms him from his sleep of death; it makes hell for a man instead of a life of peace. "Think not that I am come to send peace on earth: I came not to send peace, but a sword" (Matt. x. 34). Wherever Jesus comes He reveals that man is away from God by reason of sin, and he is terrified at His presence. That is why men will put anything in the place of Jesus Christ, anything rather than let God come near in His startling purity, because immediately God comes near, conscience records that God is holy and nothing unholy can live with Him, consequently His presence hurts the sinner. "If I had not come and spoken unto them, they had not had sin: but now they have no cloke for their sin" (John xv. 22).

(a) *Self-Consciousness.* The first thing conscience does is to rouse up self-consciousness, and that produces embarrassment. A little child is full of winsome beauty because he is utterly free from self-consciousness; when he begins to be conscious of himself he becomes awkward and shy and does all kinds of affected things; and when once the conscience of man is roused by the presence of God, it produces a consciousness of self that makes us scuttle out of His presence like bats out of the light. Most of us know much too little about what conscience succeeds in doing when we stand in the presence of God. We talk much too lightly about sin. Stand one second in the presence of God, in the light of conscience with the Spirit of God illuminating it, without Jesus Christ, and instantly you are conscious of what is stated in Genesis iii. **7**, viz. your kinship with the brute creation, with no God-quality in you.

(b) *World-Consciousness.* One effect of the disturbance caused by the light of conscience is to drive us into the outside hubbub of things. In the early days of Christianity men brooded on their sins, nowadays psychologists tell us the more wholesome way is to forget all about sin—fling yourself into the work of the world. Rushing into work in order to deaden conscience is characteristic of the life we live to-day. 'Live the simple life; keep a healthy body; never let your conscience be disturbed; for any sake keep away from religious meetings; don't bring before us the morbid tendency of things.' We shall find that the morbid tendency of things is the conviction of the Holy Ghost.

(c) *God-Consciousness.* The consciousness of God will break out in spite of all our sense of uncleanness, in spite of all our rush and interest in the work of the world, and in spite of all our logic, the implicit sense of God will come and disturb our peace.

We are laying down the fundaments of the way God has constituted man. God is holy, therefore nothing that does not partake of His holiness can abide in His presence, and that means pain. When conscience begins to be awakened by God, we either become subtle hypocrites or saints, that is, either we let God's law working through conscience bring us to the place where we can be put right, or we begin to hoodwink ourselves, to affect a religious pose, not before other people, but before ourselves, in order to appease conscience—anything to be kept out of the real presence of God because wherever He comes, He disturbs.

(3) THE AWAKENING OF CONSCIENCE.

(a) *Armoured in Sin.* The majority of men are dead in trespasses and sins. Our Lord illustrates this—"When a strong man armed keepeth his palace, his goods are in peace: but when a stronger than he shall come upon him, and overcome him, he taketh from him all his armour wherein he

63

trusted, and divideth his spoils" (Luke xi. 21–2). When the prince of this world rules, men are armoured in sin, not necessarily in wrongdoing, but in a wrong attitude, consequently they have no disturbance, no trouble, no perplexity. As the Psalmist says, "They are not in trouble as other men; they have more than heart could wish. . . . There are no pangs in their death" (Ps. lxxiii. 4–7).

(b) *Awakened in Sin.* How is conscience in men like that to be awakened? No man can awaken another man; the Spirit of God alone can awaken him. Our Lord did not say that the strong man *battles* with the stronger man: He says, "When a stronger than he shall come, and *overcome* him . . ." When once the Spirit of God shows Jesus Christ to a man in that condition, his armour is gone, and he experiences distress and pain and upset, exactly as Jesus said he would. Before, he had been armoured with the peace of the prince of this world and his conscience recorded that everything was all right. Immediately Jesus Christ is presented, conscience records what the man is in the light of God, and the garrison within is disturbed, his peace and joy are gone, and he is under what is called conviction of sin.

(c) *Awakening to Holiness.* "And when He is come He will convict of sin." We are apt to put conviction of sin in the wrong place in a man's life. The man of all men who experienced conviction of sin was the saintly apostle Paul. "For I was alive without the law once: but when the commandment came, sin revived, and I died" (Rom. vii. 9). There is no mention of conviction of sin in Paul's account of his conversion, only conviction of darkness and distress and of being out of order. But after Paul had been three years in Arabia with the Holy Ghost blazing through him, he began to write the diagnoses of sin which we have in his Epistles. The sense of sin is in proportion to the sense of holiness. The hymn has it rightly—

> And they who fain would serve Thee best
> Are conscious most of wrong within.

It does not mean that indwelling sin and indwelling holiness

64

abide together: indwelling sin can never abide with indwelling holiness; it means exactly what Paul said, "I know that in me (that is, in my flesh) dwelleth no good thing . . ." (Rom. vii. 18). "But we had the sentence of death in ourselves, that we should not trust in ourselves . . ." (2 Cor. i. 9). The majority of us have caught on the jargon of holiness without the tremendous panging pain that follows the awakening to holiness. The Spirit of God brings us to face ourselves steadily in the light of God until sin is seen in its true nature. If you want to know what sin is, don't ask the convicted sinner, ask the saint, the one who has been awakened to the holiness of God through the Atonement; he is the one who can begin to tell you what sin is. The man writhing at the penitent form is affected because his sins have upset him, but he has very little knowledge of sin. It is only as we walk in the light as God is in the light that we begin to understand the unfathomable depths of cleansing to which the blood of Jesus Christ goes (1 John i. 7). Every now and again the Spirit of God allows the saint to look back as the apostle Paul did when he said, "I was before a blasphemer, and a persecutor, and injurious." Paul was a mature saint at this time, but he is looking back into what he was before Jesus Christ apprehended him.

Conscience is the internal perception of God's moral law. Have you ever been convicted of sin by conscience through the Spirit of God? If you have, you know this—that God dare not forgive you and be God. There is a lot of sentimental talk about God forgiving because He is love: God is so holy that He cannot forgive. God can only destroy for ever the thing that is unlike Himself. The Atonement does not mean that God forgives a sinner and allows him to go on sinning and receiving forgiveness; it means that God saves the sinner and turns him into a saint, i.e. destroys the sinner out of him, and through his conscience he realizes that by the Atonement God has done what He never could have done apart from it. When people testify you can always tell whether they have been convicted by the Spirit of God or whether their equilibrium has been disturbed by doing wrong things. When a man is convicted of sin by the Spirit of God through his conscience, his relationship to other people is absolute child's play. If when you were convicted of sin, you had been told to go and lick the dust off the boots of your greatest enemy, you would have done it willingly. Your relationship to men is the last thing that bothers you. It is your relationship to God that bothers you. I am completely out of the love of God, out of the holiness of God, and I tremble with terror when I think of God drawing near. That is the real element of conviction of sin, and it is one of the rarest things nowadays because men are not uplifting the white light of Jesus Christ upon God, they are uplifting arbitrary standards of right. They are uplifting, for instance, the conduct of man to man; they are telling us we should love our fellow men. The consequence is the majority of us get off scot-free, we begin to feel very self-righteous, ". . . but they *comparing themselves among themselves*, are not wise." But when conscience is illuminated by the Holy Ghost, these three amazing articles —God is Love, God is Holy, God is Near—are brought straight down to our inner life and we can neither look up nor down for terror. When a man begins his life with God there are great tracts of his life that he never bothers his head about, but slowly and surely the Spirit of God educates him down to the tiny little scruple. Every crook and cranny of the physical life, every imagination and emotion is perfectly known to God, and He demands that all these be blameless. That brings us to absolute despair unless Jesus Christ can do what He claims He can. The marvel of the Atonement is just this very thing, that the perfect Saviour imparts His perfections to me, and as I walk in the light as God is in the light, every part of bodily life, of affectionate life and of spirit life are kept unblameable in holiness; my duty is to keep in the light, God does all the rest. That is why the life of God within the saint produces agony every now and again, because God won't leave us alone, He won't say, 'Now that will do.' He will keep at us, blazing and burning us, He is a 'consuming fire.' That phrase becomes

66

the greatest consolation we ever had. God will consume and shake, and shake and consume, till there is nothing more to be consumed, but only Himself—incandescent with the presence of God.

HUMANITY

Psalm ii.

"God does His business, do yours" (*Amiel*).

The tendency nowadays is to take the management of the universe out of God's hands, while at the same time neglecting our business, viz. the government of our own universe within.

(1) ENTHUSIASM FOR HUMANITY. *v.* 2.

The main line indicated in the Bible with regard to the human race and God's purpose for it is that God allows the human race full liberty, and He allows the spirit of evil, viz. Satan, nearly full liberty also. Peter says that God is long-suffering (2 Peter iii. 9); He is giving us ample opportunity to try whatever line we like both in individual and in national life, but the Bible reveals that in the final end of all things, men will confess that God's purpose and His judgment are right. We must disabuse our minds of the idea that God sits like a Judge on a throne and batters humanity into shape. He is sometimes presented in that way, not intentionally, but simply because the majority of people have forgotten the principle laid down by Jesus, that "there is nothing covered that shall not be revealed; and hid, that shall not be known"; and that in the end, God's judgments will be made utterly plain and clear, and men will agree that they are right. Meantime, God is giving humanity and the devil ample opportunity to try and prove that His purposes and His judgments are wrong.

Enthusiasm means intensity of interest. Enthusiasm for Humanity is one thing; enthusiasm for saints is another, God's purpose is the latter. In order that we may see exactly the forces and the problems that are at work morally, we will look at these heads:

(*a*) *The Master Man* (Romans v. 12). Adam stands as the

Federal Head of the race, he is the master key to the virtues that still remain in sinful men. These virtues must be understood as remnants left of God's original design, and not promises of what man is going to be. The moral problem comes in this way: we inherit by nature certain strong cardinal virtues, but these are not the slightest atom of use to us, and when a man or woman is born again of the Spirit of God, these virtues are nearly always a hindrance instead of a benefit. Think of the virtues which Jesus Christ demands in His teaching and compare them with the cardinal virtues left in us as the remnants of a ruined manhood, not as promises of the new manhood, and you will see why it is that we cannot patch up our natural virtues to come anywhere near Jesus Christ's demands. We must be re-made on the inside and develop new virtues entirely, 'a new man in Christ Jesus.' This is one part of the problem which no teacher outside the Bible deals with. Books on ethics and morals take the natural virtues as promises of what a man is going to be; the Bible indicates that they are remnants of what man once was, and the key to these virtues is Adam, not Jesus Christ. This accounts for our Lord's attitude, a strange perplexing attitude until we understand this point. Jesus loves the natural virtues, and yet He refers to them in a way which makes them seem utterly futile. Take the natural virtues in the rich young ruler, we read that Jesus looking on him, "loved him." Natural virtues are beautiful in the sight of Jesus, but He knows as none other could know, that they are not promises of what man is going to be, but remnants, 'trailing clouds of glory,' left in man, and are not of the slightest atom of practical use to him. Jesus Christ told the rich young ruler that he must strip himself of all he possessed, give his manhood to Him and then come and follow Him; in other words he must be re-made entirely.

(*b*) *The Muddle of Men* (Romans v. 12). The 'muddle of men' refers to the whole of the human race since Adam; we are all a muddle, "for that all have sinned." Since Adam, men, individually and collectively, present a muddle morally which has puzzled everyone; the Bible is the only Book that tells us how the moral muddle has been produced, viz. by sin. In those in whom the cardinal virtues are strong and clear, there is another element which the Bible calls sin (no one else calls it sin), and it is this element which makes men and women a complete muddle; you do not know how to sort them out. In some particulars they are good, and in others they are bad, and the problem arises when you fix on one point of their personality as if it were the only point. For example, when Oscar Wilde wrote "De Profundis" in prison, he allowed one point of his personality to have way, viz. his sentimental intellectual interest in Jesus Christ, and the book was written from that point of view. He wrote sincerely, but he overlooked all the other points of his personality which contradicted that particular one, and when he came out of prison it was those other points that dominated. That is what we mean by 'the muddle of men,' and everyone who touches it, outside the Bible, instead of clearing it up makes it worse. The muddle is explained by one word: sin.

(c) *The Mystery Man* (2 Thessalonians ii. 3–4). The Bible reveals that the sin which muddles men and society is ultimately going to appear in an incarnation called the man of sin, or the Antichrist. The enthusiasm of humanity for itself in its present state simply means irrevocable disaster ultimately. Nowadays people talk about the whole human race being in the making, that our natural virtues are promises of what we are going to be; they take no account at all of sin. We have to remember that an enthusiasm for humanity which ignores the Bible is sure to end in disaster; enthusiasm for the community of saints means that God can take hold of the muddle and can re-make men, not simply in accordance with the Master man before the fall, but "conformed to the image of His Son" (Romans viii. 29).

(2) THE EMBARRASSMENT OF HUMANITY. *vv.* 4–6.

(a) *Bastard Solidarity* (Genesis vi. 5; Hebrews xii. 8). Solidarity means consolidation and oneness of interest, the solidarity of the human race means that every member of the race has one point of interest with every other member. Notice how the whole of Scripture is knit together over this false solidarity of sin. It is quite possible for the human mind to blot God out of its thinking entirely, and to work along the line of the elements which are the same in every man, and to band the whole of the human race into a solid atheistic community. The only reason this has not been done up to the present is that the human race has been too much divided, but we shall find that these divisions are gradually resolving themselves. There are elements in human nature that are the same in everybody, and if once the human mind succeeded in obliterating God, the whole of the human race would become one vast phalanx of atheism.

(b) *Babel of Souls* (Genesis xi. 1-9). This is the first time solidarity was attempted, away in hoary antiquity. What encumbers and embarrasses humanity is an uncomfortable feeling that God is laughing at them all the time, and in the history of men up to the present time the hindrance to perfectly organized atheism has been the saints who represent the derision of God: if they were removed, we should find perfectly organized atheism.

(c) *Body of sin* (Romans vi. 6). The body of sin is this tremendous possibility of solid atheism underlying humanity; the share of individual men and women in that body is called 'the old man.' Every time a man or woman by identification with Jesus enters into the experimental knowledge that his 'old man' is crucified with Christ, the ultimate defeat and destruction of the body of sin becomes clearer. The body of sin is not in a man; what is in a man is 'the old man,' the carnal mind, which connects him with the body of sin. The solidarity of sin forms the basis of the power of Satan, and it runs all through humanity, making it possible for the whole human race to be atheistic. Sin in its beginning is simply being without God. Paul's argument is that the purpose of 'the old man' being crucified with Christ, is that the body of sin might be destroyed, i.e. that the connection with the body of sin might be severed. Everyone who becomes identified with the death of Jesus

Christ aims another blow at Satan and at the great solidarity of sin. There are two mystical bodies—there is the mystical body of Christ, and the mystical body of sin which is anticipated in the man of sin. When a man begins to go wrong, he says, 'I can't help it'; perfectly true. God's Book reveals the great oracle of evil, the tremendous power behind wrongdoing; it is a supernatural power antagonistic to God. We do not battle against flesh and blood, but "against principalities, against powers, against the rulers of the darkness of this world, against spiritual wickedness in high places." When a man is saved and sanctified, he is severed from the body of sin, and consequently all the powers of darkness backed by Satan make a dead set for that soul. The only thing that can keep a sanctified soul is the almighty power of God through Jesus Christ, but kept by that power he is perfectly safe. When once the saints are removed, the world will be faced with the menace of the solidarity of sin and atheism.

"The question of the moment is: A God that serves Humanity, or a Humanity that serves God?" (Forsyth). When men depart from the Bible they call humanity 'God' in differing terms; the use of the term 'God' means nothing to them, God is simply the name given to the general tendencies which further men's interests. This spirit is honeycombing everything, we find it coming into the way we talk of Christian experience; there is creeping in the idea that God and Jesus Christ and the Holy Ghost are simply meant to bless us, to further our interests. When we come to the New Testament we find exactly the opposite idea, that by regeneration we are brought into such harmony and union with God that we realize with great joy that we are meant to serve His interests.

(3) THE EMBROILMENT OF HUMANITY. *vv.* 7–9.

Embroilment means to involve in perplexity. It is the presence of the saints that upsets the calculations of Satan; and it is the presence of Jesus that involves not only Satan but humanity in all kinds of distractions. If men and Satan could only get rid of Jesus Christ, they would never be involved in perplexity, never be upset. Jesus put it very clearly: "If I had not come and spoken unto them, they had not had sin: but now they have no cloke for their sin" (John xv. 22). The greatest annoyance to Satan and to humanity is Jesus Christ. Twenty centuries ago the Apostle John wrote, "every spirit which confesseth not Jesus" (R.V. 'annulleth Jesus'—dissolves Jesus by analysis) "is not of God; and this is the spirit of the Antichrist, whereof ye have heard that it cometh" (1 John iv. 3). Watch the tendency abroad to-day; people want to get rid of Jesus Christ, they cannot prove that He did not live, or that He was not a remarkable Man; but they set to work to dissolve Him by analysis, to say He was not really God Incarnate. Jesus Christ always upsets the calculations of humanity; that is what made Voltaire say 'Crucify the wretch, stamp Him and His crazy tale out,' because He was the stumbling-block to all the reasonings of men. You cannot work Jesus Christ into any system of thinking. If you could keep Him out, everything could be explained. The world could be explained by evolution, but you cannot fit Jesus Christ into the theory of evolution. Jesus Christ is an annoyance to Satan, a thorn in the side of the world at large, an absolute distress to sin in the individual. If we could crucify Him and stamp Him out, the annoyance would cease. In dealing with the carnal mind, Paul says it is *"enmity against God."*

(*a*) *The Past Watchword*—a religion that utilizes humanity. The error in the past on the part of religious teachers has been to present God as a great sovereign power Who utilizes humanity without rhyme or reason.

(*b*) *The Present Watchword*—a humanity that utilizes God— is the opposite, viz. that God is a great aimless, loving tendency that humanity utilizes to forgive itself, to cleanse itself, and to justify itself.

(*c*) *The Persistent Word*—a Christ that unites God and Man in love—through both the errors is this, the Lord Jesus Christ, Who can unite a holy God and an un-holy humanity by means of His wonderful Redemption. In this connection, Jesus Christ stands as the type of man, and the only type of

73

man, who can come near to God. "Christ is for the central figure of a glorified humanity to develop by Christ's aid the innate spiritual resources of a splendid race." Jesus Christ is the One Who has the power to impart His own innate spiritual life, viz. Holy Spirit, to unholy men, and develop them until they are like Himself. That is why the devil hates Jesus Christ, and why he tries to make men calculate without Him.

(4) THE EMANCIPATION OF HUMANITY. *vv.* 10–12.

When any sinful man accepts morally the verdict of God on sin in the cross of Christ, he becomes emancipated. A moral decision is different from a mental decision, which may be largely sentiment. A moral decision means—' My God, I accept Thy verdict against sin on the cross of Jesus Christ, and I want the disposition of sin in me identified with His death'—immediately a man gets there, all that we understand by the Holy Ghost working in His tremendous power through the Redemption takes place, and the emancipation of humanity is furthered. "Christ is for the central figure of a glorious God, and Humanity's chief end is to develop from reconciliation, redemption, and subjection to God's will."

(*a*) *The Second Man* (2 Corinthians v. 17–19). God emancipates the human race through this second Man, the Lord Jesus Christ. That is why Paul called Jesus Christ 'the last Adam.' If the first Adam is the key to the muddle of men, Jesus Christ, the last Adam, is the key to the emancipation of men. Jesus Christ stands for all that a man should be, and to the saints He stands for all that God is.

(*b*) *Sanctified Men* (Ephesians ii. 1–10). A sanctified man has not only had the disposition of sin crucified, but he is emancipated from his connection with the body of sin and is lifted to the heavenly places where Jesus lived when He was here. This marvellous revelation is summed up in 1 John i. 7, "But if we walk in the light, as He is in the light, we have fellowship one with another, and the blood of Jesus Christ His Son cleanseth us from all sin." This is the enthusiasm for the communion of saints in contrast to the enthusiasm for humanity. It is by thinking along these lines that we are enabled to prove experimentally what we know in our minds; and we should live with far greater power if only we would let our 'pure minds be stirred up by way of remembrance' (2 Peter iii. 1). While we are on this earth, living in alien territory, it is a marvellous emancipation to know that we are raised above it all through Jesus Christ, and that we have power over all the power of the enemy in and through Him.

(c) *Supreme Mystery* (Ephesians v. 32). Around the saints is the great power of God which keeps watch and ward over them so that 'that wicked one toucheth them not.' What is true of saints individually is true of all saints collectively, viz. that the elements which under Satan make for the solidarity of atheism, make for the solidarity of holiness under God. "Fear not, little flock; for it is your Father's good pleasure to give you the kingdom," a tiny insignificant crowd in every age. Christianity has always been a forlorn hope because the saints are in alien territory; but it is all right, God is working out His tremendous purpose for the overthrow of everything Satan and sin can do. "He that sitteth in the heavens shall laugh." Everything that sin and Satan have ruined is going to be reconstructed and readjusted through the marvellous Redemption of our Lord Jesus Christ.

HARMONY

(1) HEALTH—PHYSICAL HARMONY. (*Genesis* ii. 1–9, 15–17.)
   Peace of Fact.

Harmony means a fitting together of parts so as to form a
connected whole, agreement in relation.   Health, or physical
harmony, is God's plan from the very beginning.   The first
mention of any subject in the Book of Genesis colours
every allusion to that subject throughout the Bible.   Health
(physical harmony), Happiness (moral harmony) and Holiness (spiritual harmony) are all divergent views as to what
is the main aim of a man's life.   Health, or physical harmony, is a perfect balance between our organism and the
outer world.

(*a*) *The Cult of the Splendid Animal.* (Psalm cxlvii. 10.)
There always have been and always will be people who
worship splendid, well-groomed health.   This verse reveals
that God places health, or physical harmony, in a totally
different relationship from that which it is put in by man.
The modern name for the worship of physical health is
Christian Science.   The great error of the healthy-minded
cult is that it ignores a man's moral and spiritual life.

(*b*) *The Cult of the Sick Attitude.* (Psalm xxxix. 6–11.)
A great many people indulge in the luxury of misery; their
one worship is of anguish, agony, weakness and sensitiveness
to pain.   The cult of the sick attitude is well established
in human history by the fact that most of the great men
and women whose personalities have marked the life of their
time have been to some degree deranged physically.   Amiel,
a highly sensitive and cultured man, almost too morbid
to exist, was a lifelong invalid, and he wrote thus in his
Journal: "The first summonses of illness have a divine
value, so that evils though they seem, they are really an
appeal to us from on high, a touch of God's Fatherly
scourge."   The healthy-minded people do not agree with

that attitude, and sick people are inclined to worship it. The attitude to sickness in the Bible is totally different from the attitude of people who believe in faith-healing. The Bible attitude is not that God sends sickness or that sickness is of the devil, but that sickness is a fact usable by both God and the devil. Never base a principle on your own experience. My personal experience is this: I have never once in my life been sick without being to blame for it. As soon as I turned my mind to asking why the sickness was allowed, I learned a lesson that I have never forgotten, viz. that my physical health depends absolutely on my relationship to God. Never pin your faith to a doctrine or to anyone else's statement, get hold of God's Book, and you will find that your spiritual character determines exactly how God deals with you personally. People continually get into fogs because they will not take God's line, they will take someone else's line. God's Book deals with facts. Health and sickness are facts, not fancies. There are cases recorded in the Bible, and in our own day, of people who have been marvellously healed, for what purpose? For us to imitate them? Never, but in order that we might discern what lies behind, viz. the individual relationship to a personal God. The peace arising from fact is unintelligent and dangerous, e.g. people who base on the fact of health are at peace, but it is often a peace which makes them callous. On the other hand, people who accept the fact of being sick are inclined to have a jaundiced eye for everything healthy. For a man to make health his god is to put himself merely at the head of the brute creation.

I am purposely leaving the subject vague and without an answer; there can be no answer. The great difficulty is that people find answers which they say came from God. You cannot prove facts; you have to swallow them. The fact of health and the fact of sickness are there; we have nothing to do with choosing them, they come and go. We have to get on to another platform, the moral platform, and then the spiritual platform, before we can begin to get an explanation of these facts.

(2) HAPPINESS—MORAL HARMONY. *Peace of Principle.*

Happiness or moral harmony is a perfect balance between our inclination and our environment. The peace of principle keeps a man's moral nature in a state of harmony.

(a) *Pride of Integrity.* (Luke xviii. 11.) Integrity means the unimpaired state of anything, and pride in the integrity of a man or woman's morality will produce happiness. They have no need of prayer, or if they do pray it is a soliloquy of peace before high heaven. The Pharisee in Our Lord's parable was happy; he was not praying to God, or that others might hear; he was praying "with himself,"—"God, I thank Thee that I am not as other men are, extortioners, unjust, adulterers, or even as this publican." Look at him, then put your own name behind him and you have got his portrait exactly; you know where he lives and everything about him. Beware of calling this type of happiness self-righteousness; the phrase which gives the true meaning would be 'happy satisfaction with my intellectual and moral conduct.' That happiness is impregnable to God and to the devil; its true emblem is ice. If you want to find an analysis of every kind of moral and immoral character, the Bible is the place to look for it. This picture in Luke xviii. is not the picture of a man of the world, but of a religious man. As Christians we have to beware of Pharisaic holiness along the line of sanctification.

(b) *The Pain of Iniquity.* (Luke xviii. 13.) This is the stage when the peace of principle has broken down. "When Thou with rebukes doth correct man for iniquity, Thou makest his beauty consume away like a moth" (Psalm xxxix. 11). According to the steadily reiterated teachings of Jesus Christ, a man who is in moral harmony with himself without being rightly related to Jesus Christ, is much nearer the devil than a bad-living man.

Harmony, both physical and moral, is God-ordained, i.e. it is God's will that a man's body with all its component parts should be in perfect harmony with themselves and with the outer world, and it is God's will that a man should be in moral harmony with himself and happy in that sense;

and yet, as we have pointed out, the Bible reveals that a man can have physical health at the cost of his moral welfare, and happiness at the cost of spiritual welfare.

(3) HOLINESS—SPIRITUAL HARMONY.   *Peace of God.*

Holiness, or spiritual harmony, is a perfect balance between our disposition and all the law of God.   Never trust your temperament, i.e. your sensibility to things.   When God makes a saint He plants a new disposition in him, but He does not alter his temperament; the saint has to mould his temperament according to the new disposition. Take your own experience, think of the time before you knew God, before God gave you the Holy Spirit, before you entered into the life of sanctification, your temperament and your sensibilities produced in you a horror for certain things which now you look at from a totally different attitude, and you begin to say, 'Why, I must be getting callous!' Nothing of the sort, you have a new disposition with which your temperament is being brought into harmony, and that disposition being God-given is bringing you into sympathy with God's way of looking at things so that you are no longer the creature of your sensibilities.   If you have begun to get discouraged over the difficulty of disciplining your sensibilities, don't be discouraged, get at it again.   At the beginning we are apt to be tripped up by our sensibilities because they have not yet been brought into complete subjection to the Lord Jesus Christ.   Remember, although Jesus Christ is on the throne, you are 'prime minister' under Him.

(*a*) *Untouched by Panic*.   (Psalm cxii. 7.)   Our Lord never suffered from physical or moral or intellectual panics, because He was fixed in God.   "But Jesus did not commit Himself unto them, because He knew all men, . . . for He knew what was in man" (John ii. 24, 25).   Look at your own experience and see how your sensibilities will run you into panics and try and make you believe a lie.   It is through their sensibilities that Satan tries to get hold of the saints. God said to Satan about Job, "Behold, all that he hath

is in thy hand; only upon himself put not forth thine hand"
(Job i. 12). For our present argument may this not mean
that Satan cannot touch the ruling disposition; but that
if we are not on the watch at all the loopholes, he will get
hold of the sensibilities and try to bring us into bondage?
Whenever you feel bondage spiritually, smell brimstone, you
are on a wrong tack. Panics are always wrong, there is
nothing in them. What a blessing it is to know someone
who never gets into a panic! someone you can always depend
on. You go to them in a flurry, with fired and jangled
nerves, brain like cotton-wool, heart panting like a butterfly
nearly dead, and in two or three minutes everything is
quietened. What has happened? The difference in you has
come about because that one is paying no attention to
his sensibilities but only to the one bed-rock reality of
the life, viz. God. Holiness is untouched by panic. "In
tumults oft," says Paul. What is a tumult? Watch a
porridge-pot boiling, that is a tumult; to be inside that,
undisturbed, means something, and that type of character
is the only one that can stand as a worker for God in this
world. A man or woman with that disposition in them can
stand where Jesus Christ stood, because it is His own disposition that is in them, and that disposition cannot be
upset, it cannot be made to take account of the evil. In
the eyes of the world the way a saint trusts God is always
absurd, until there is trouble on, then the world is inclined
to kneel down and worship the saint.

(b) *Undeterred by Persecution.* (Psalm cxii. 10.) God's
Book reveals all through that holiness will bring persecution
from those who are not holy. Our Lord taught His disciples
to be conspicuous. "Ye are the light of the world"; "a
city that is set on a hill"; and He taught them never to
hide the truth for fear of wolfish men. (Matthew x. 16.)
Personal experience bears out the truth that a testimony
to holiness produces either rage or ridicule on the part of
those who are not holy. We are all cowards naturally;
we are only not cowards when God has altered our disposition, because the disposition God puts in keeps us fixed

in a right relationship to Himself. The one dominant note
of the life of a saint is first of all sympathy with God and
God's ideas, not with human beings. A twofold line runs
all through God's Book, and especially in the Epistles of
St. Paul, with regard to public preaching and teaching and
dealing with people in private: Be as stern and unflinching
as God Almighty in your preaching, but as tender and
gentle as a sinner saved by grace should be when you deal
with a human soul. To-day the order is being reversed and
modern teaching is amazingly 'easy-osy.' Look at the
standard of the preaching of to-day; sympathy with human
beings is put first, not sympathy with God, and the truth
of God is withheld. It must be withheld, it dare not be
preached, because immediately the fullness of a personal
salvation is preached—which means I must be right with
God, must have a disposition which is in perfect harmony
with God's laws and which will enable me to work them
out, it produces conviction and resentment and upset. Jesus
Christ taught His disciples never to keep back the truth
of God for fear of persecution. When we come to dealing
with our fellow-men, what is our attitude to be? Remember
yourself, remember who you are, and that if you have
attained to anything in the way of holiness, remember Who
made you what you are. "But by the grace of God I am
what I am," says the Apostle Paul (1 Cor. xv. 10). Deal
with infinite pity and sympathy with other souls, keeping
your eye on what you once were and what, by the grace
of God, you are now.

In dealing with yourself be as patient as God is with
you. Beware of the spiritual sulks which spring from thinking that because I, a two-year-old in sanctifying grace, am
not as big and mature and strong as the twenty-year-old
in grace, I can't be sanctified rightly! There is more danger
there than most saints think. (See Hebrews xii. 5–11.)
The devil tries to make us think that when we have entered
into the sanctified life, all is done; it is only begun. We
have entered into Jesus Christ's finished work, but remember,
says Paul, you have attained to nothing yet; everything is

perfectly adjusted, now begin to attain and to "grow up into Him in all things."

These three things develop slowly together: first, the basis of spiritual holiness; second, the building of moral happiness; and third, the decoration of physical health. A full-grown man in Christ Jesus is one who has become exactly like Christ Jesus. "Till we all come . . . unto the measure of the stature of the fullness of Christ" (Eph. iv. 13).